OPENING CRED

CW00385742

Contributors this issue: James Aaron, Simon J. Ballard, Rachel Bellwoar, David Michael Brown, James Cadman, Martin Dallard, David Flack, John Harrison, Julian Hobbs, Kev Hurst, Bryan C. Kuriawa, James Lecky, Allen Rubinstein, Peter Sawford, Ian Talbot Taylor, Dr Andrew C. Webber. Caricature artwork by Aaron Stielstra.

All articles, photographs and specially produced artwork remain copyright their respective author/photographer/artist. Opinions expressed herein are those of the individual.

Design and Layout: Dawn Dabell
Copy Editor: Jonathon Dabell

A Word from the Editing Room

Welcome back!

We're delighed to bring you Issue 9 of 'Cinema of the '70s', containing articles on the likes of *Duel, Capricorn One, The Great Waldo Pepper, Assault on Precinct 13, 1941, 10 Rillington Place, Beyond the Valley of the Dolls* and much more. We also have an extensive overview of the screen career of the late Raquel Welch.

Readers may have noticed that for the first time since launching this magazine, there has been an increase to the cover price. Each copy we sell is printed on demand by Amazon KDP, in or close to the destination country. This is a useful arrangement which enables us to reach readers in all corners of the world without incurring expensive international postage or having to predict bulk printing quantities. However, the Amazon KDP service raised its opearting costs from 20th June 2023 due to rising global prices. We were left with a choice between raising our own cover price or ceasing to produce the publications altogether. We've taken the unwanted decision to charge more; we hope our readers will stick with us and continue to support this labour of love magazine.

That's enough about the economics of it all. What we're really here for is to discuss the stars and movies of the '70s. A point worth mentioning is that considerable controversy erupted recently when the Criterion Channel censored a scene from *The French Connection* without warning or explanation, prompting angry responses from fans of the film. There is an increasing risk, a likelihood even, that films from the past could find themselves on the receiving end of such censorship. Questionable sexual attitudes, casual racial slurs, offhand prejudices, etc, can be found in many films from eras past. But is it acceptable to tinker with such products in an attempt to make them more palatable to modern sensibilities? Should art in any form be altered by other hands? A fascinating question and, perhaps, the start of a slippery slope!

Until next time, happy reading!

Dawn and Jonathon Dabell.

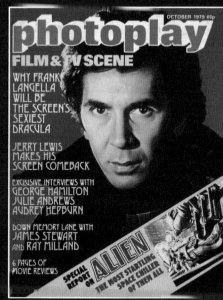

Remembering Jim Brown (1936-2023)

On May 18th, 2023, Jim Brown died at his home in Los Angeles at the age of 87. The cause of death was stated as natural causes. He'd first found fame and success as a football player, playing fullback for the Cleveland Browns from 1957 until 1965. He broke various records during his playing career.

He began acting in 1964 and quickly amassed several impressive screen credits in the '60s, becoming one of the most popular black actors in the business. Key roles included *The Dirty Dozen* (1967), *Dark of the Sun* (1968), *Ice Station Zebra* (1968) and *100 Rifles* (1969). His busiest decade was the '70s where he enjoyed particular success in the blaxploitation genre.

His complete '70s filmography is as follows:

...tick ...tick... tick (1970)
El Condor (1970)
The Grasshopper (1970)
Slaughter (1972)
Black Gunn (1972)
Slaughter's Big Rip-Off (1973)
The Slams (1973)
I Escaped from Devil's Island (1974)
Three the Hard Way (1974)
Take a Hard Ride (1975)
Kid Vengeance (1977)
Fingers (1978)
Pacific Inferno (1978)

Rest well, Mr. Brown.
You will be missed. Thanks for the memories.

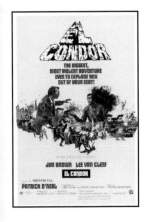   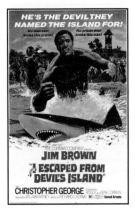 

In Memoriam

Harry Belafonte
(1927-2023)
Actor, known for *The Angel Levine* (1970) and *Buck and the Preacher* (1972).

Helmut Berger
(1944-2023)
Actor, known for *The Garden of the Finzi-Continis* (1970) and *Salon Kitty* (1976).

Robert Blake
(1933-2023)
Actor, known for *Electra Glide in Blue* (1973) and *Busting* (1974).

Andrés Garcia
(1941-2023)
Actor, known for *Tintorera* (1977) and *Cyclone* (1978).

Barry Humphries
(1934-2023)
Actor, known for *The Adventures of Barry Mackenzie* (1972) and *Barry Mackenzie Holds His Own* (1974).

Murray Melvin
(1932-2023)
Actor, known for *The Devils* (1971) and *Barry Lyndon* (1974).

Barry Newman
(1930-2023)
Actor, known for *Vanishing Point* (1971) and *Fear is the Key* (1972).

Stella Stevens
(1938-2023)
Actress, known for *The Poseidon Adventure* (1972) and *Las Vegas Lady* (1975).

Topol
(1935-2023)
Actor, known for *Fiddler on the Roof* (1971) and *Follow Me* (1972).

Treat Williams
(1951-2023)
Actor, known for *The Eagle Has Landed* (1976) and *Hair* (1979).

STEVEN SPIELBERG'S DUEL
Mann, You Need Help

by James Aaron

For more than fifty years, film lovers and pop culture warriors alike have looked back at Steven Spielberg's *Duel* as the film that introduced movie audiences to the man who would become a legend. And what a debut it was: taut and efficient in construction, assured and effective in execution. Ninety minutes of nonstop cat-and-mouse between one man and his merciless pursuer. Yet there is more to the movie that just one extended car chase. *Duel* is not just a *Jaws* progenitor - as it is often described (frankly not without merit) - but also an introduction to the personal themes to which Spielberg would return throughout his career: isolation, loneliness and the breakup of the nuclear family.

Although *Duel* has long been recognized as the official arrival of Spielberg as a bona fide filmmaker, it didn't start that way. Despite all its polish and obvious cinematic potential, the movie initially served as just another step in the director's blossoming television career. Coming on the heels of helming stints on popular series like *Columbo*, *Night Gallery* and *Marcus Welby, M.D.*, the director's first full-length movie debut on November 13, 1971 actually took place on American television as the ABC Movie of the Week. There, it garnered solid if not exactly world-beating ratings as the 18th highest rated TV movie that year, grabbing 33% of the television audience the night it aired at a time when television choices were far fewer than the kaleidoscopic cable and streaming hellscape of today.

Fortunately for the moviegoing public, that performance was enough to convince Universal to expand the movie into a theatrical release for Europe. The studio gave Spielberg the additional money and time required to grow the film's running time from 77 to 90 minutes, the minimum length required in those days for theatrical distribution in Europe. As a result, *Duel* gained what today are some its most pivotal scenes, including the protagonist's phone call home to his wife and a sequence where the villainous truck tries to push the hero's car into an oncoming train. With its additional minutes, in October 1972 the film hit cinemas in the United Kingdom. Several other European countries and Japan followed later in 1973. As with the TV ratings, box office was decent but didn't break any records. There was little indication of Spielbergian blockbusters to come, although it did win a couple of major awards in America - the Golden Globe for Best Movie Made for TV and an Emmy for outstanding sound editing.

Still, the groundwork was laid. Five decade's worth of success and a career as arguably the greatest film director of all time would follow in short order. Spielberg's next two films were also created for television (*Something Evil* in 1972, *Savage* in 1973) before *The Sugarland Express* hit theaters in 1974, followed of course by *Jaws* in 1975, which sent him into the stratosphere for good. We'll come back to that last one.

As directed by Spielberg, written for the screen by Richard Matheson from his novella of the same name and starring veteran character actor Dennis Weaver as nebbish suburban husband David Mann, *Duel* was in many ways the era's typical low-budget, tight-schedule TV movie. It's a simple tale: a man (er, Mann) is pursued on a desert highway by the vengeful driver of a tanker truck, after Mann delivers the egregious insult of passing the truck on the highway. No intertwined subplots, no parallel storylines playing out in far-flung locations. Just a lean and lethal thriller: man versus machine.

Shot (initially) over 13 days for a budget of $400,000, the story utilized only a handful of locations and characters to tell its tale. All but six scenes take place on the highway: the aforementioned scenes where Mann calls his wife and where he is nearly shoved into a speeding train, plus a scene where the hero stops in a diner and realizes his tormentor is there with him, and another where he tries to move a stalled school bus out of the way only to have the truck finish the job for him. There is also a stop at a gas station, and a scene that provides perhaps the movie's most iconic sequence, where Mann pulls over to seek help and use the phone at a roadside snake show and culminates with Mann escaping the phone booth barely a moment before the truck slams through the little

structure, blowing it apart like driftwood. Since the phone call, train track and school bus scenes were added later for the theatrical release, that means only three scenes were originally planned and shot off the road.

Save for a brief opening sequence showing Weaver's character driving out of the city and out into the scrubby desert landscape, the rest of the movie is Mann against the driver. Virtually every frame - on road or off - is shot clear through with suspense. Where miles of desert highway could easily feel tedious in lesser hands, Spielberg and his team never allow boredom to settle into the proceedings. Through masterful editing and sound design, the movie never loses its momentum. Each scene builds on the last and hurtles forward into the next.

Yet even at that breakneck pace, *Duel* finds moments for character development. Spielberg nods to some themes he would return to in future classics. The obsessive paranoia of *Close Encounters of the Third Kind*, *Jaws* and *Munich* runs most prominently throughout the story. Sometimes the paranoia comes from brief, quiet scenes involving Mann's own inner monologue, expressed in voice-over as he tries to understand his attacker's motives. More overtly, the sequence in Chuck's Diner where Mann tries to determine which of the other patrons is his pursuer - ultimately guessing wrong - is a master class of suspicion, as he hones in on every word and minute detail of the men seated at the counter, searching for the smallest clue that

could give away his foe's identity. (This scene also features a brilliant tracking shot that follows Weaver from the diner's entrance all the way to the back restroom, staying on his shell-shocked facial expression the entire time in a masterful camera move made even more impressive by the fact that the Steadicam hadn't even been invented yet.)

Beyond paranoia, there's the breakdown of family, another recurring Spielberg theme. The director had himself lived through the divorce of his own mother and father, and that experience left a permanent impression that he revisited to great effect time and again in movies like *Close Encounters, E.T: The Extra Terrestrial, Hook, Poltergeist* (which he wrote), *War of the Worlds* and *Catch Me If You Can.* Even further, *Duel* homes in on failed masculinity as the root of the family's dysfunction. During the opening credit sequence, as Mann drives away from the city into

the desert, he sits up with perfect posture, collar buttoned down, necktie perfectly straight - a portrait of the perfect suburban family man. But on the radio, we hear a talk show where a man proclaims himself part of Richard Nixon's conservative silent majority and complains that "the day I got married was the day I lost the position as head of the family" because his wife is the family breadwinner.

Gradually from there, we witness the emasculation of our hero. Not long after that scene, just after his first encounter with the tanker truck, Mann speaks with his wife on the telephone, about his own feelings of weakness over having recently not protected her from another overly aggressive man. Later, Mann's manhood (sorry) comes into question again, when he is unsuccessful in moving the stalled school bus only to watch helplessly as the tanker truck comes up from behind and frees the vehicle with an easy push. And in truly ironic fashion, the deadly events of the story are set into motion when he actually tries to be assertive for once by passing the offensive, smoke-belching truck - only to anger the driver and put his own life at risk as a result. Another failure. It's not until Mann ultimately defeats the truck by forcing it over a cliff that he is able to regain his masculinity.

But above all, the truck and driver in *Duel* are the living embodiment of faceless fear and obsession, themes Spielberg would tackle to much greater success a couple of films later. The truck - the obsession - terrorizes out in the open, its hulking metal body careening through vehicles and phone booths in broad daylight, relentless and unbowing. But the driver - save for one moment when we see his face in the diner, full on - *or so we believe* - is never clearly seen, visible only in small glimpses: a hand here, an arm there, a partial reflection over there. That's fear - being targeted, but not being able to identify your attacker or his motives. A nameless, faceless monster, a relentless destructive force hellbent on your destruction. Remind anyone of any other Spielberg films?

It's hard to look at *Duel* without seeing the similarities to *Jaws,* which Spielberg and Universal would thrust on the world in 1975, smashing all box-office records and forever cementing the Hollywood blockbuster mindset. *Duel* features its Everyman protagonist being pursued across a desolate landscape by an unrelenting violent force. *Jaws* does the same. Just trade the vast loneliness of the Atlantic Ocean for the vast loneliness of the American desert, and monster shark for monster truck. Even the similar subtexts are there, with the breakdown of the family hovering around the edges of *Jaws* too, albeit not quite as pronounced as in *Duel*. (Interestingly, that theme is much more pronounced in Peter Benchley's 'Jaws' novel, which features a subplot that is just barely suggested in the movie, where Chief Brody's lonely wife seeks comfort in an extramarital affair with Hooper, the oceanographer). Spielberg even acknowledged the link between the two films at the time he made *Jaws*, when he inserted sound from the *Duel* truck's death throes over top of the shark's explosive finale, after Roy Scheider shoots the air cannister and the shark's remains slowly sink to the bottom of the ocean. As he has said in interviews since, it was both a nod to the thematic similarities and a 'Thank you' to *Duel* for ultimately providing him the opportunity to make *Jaws*. As such, *Duel* was the first step down the path that led to Spielberg becoming the most successful and influential moviemaker of his generation, and perhaps *any* generation. (He certainly gets my vote.) It's worth a revisit, and if you haven't seen it yet, consider it an essential piece of '70s filmmaking.

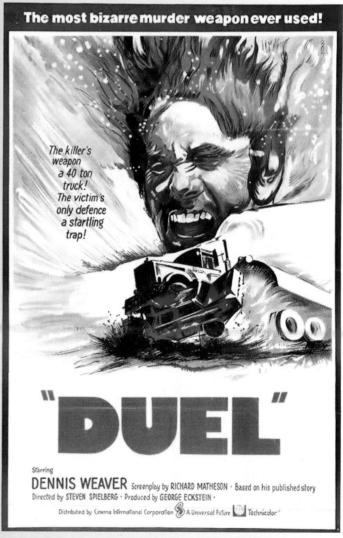

"Here They Come!"

Dr. Andrew C. Webber sizes up Raquel Welch - Last of the Bombshells

In the '70s, statuesque bombshell Raquel Welch - then in her 30s and, apparently, almost always "difficult to work with" - made an eclectic run of movies which challenged and consolidated her position as the sexiest actress on the planet. Few were big hits - some were truly dreadful and most are now long-forgotten. However, viewed over 50 years later, one thing's for sure: they don't make 'em like Raquel anymore!

In 1966, a movie poster and a few stills for the mediocre Hammer creature feature *One Million Years BC* (in which she spoke only three words) and a supporting role in Richard Fleisher's sci-fi drama *Fantastic Voyage* turned Welch almost overnight into a fur-clad love goddess who could be shrunk small enough to enter your bloodstream. There's an amusing scene in Kenneth Branagh's semi-autobiographical *Belfast* (2021) where the father chooses to take his family to the cinema to see *One Million Years,* knowing full well it will contain "something for the dads", much to the chagrin of his long-suffering wife.

Welch followed this by starring in the daft British spy comedy *Fathom* (1967) and an amusing turn (she regularly tapped into her comic, as well as her sexy, side) in Stanley Donen's *Bedazzled* (also 1967), a variant of the oft-told 'Faust' tale featuring Peter Cook and Dudley Moore (Welch, somewhat unsurprisingly, played Miss Lillian Lust). She then made a couple of half decent westerns - Andrew V. McLaglen's *Bandolero!* and Tom Gries' troubled *100 Rifles* (which included a controversial inter-racial love scene between Welch and Jim Brown, and a shower scene that ranks alongside *Psycho* in the pantheon of famous shower scenes on screen). After *100 Rifles*, Welch vowed never to work with co-star Burt Reynolds again due to their temperamental off-screen relationship. She went on to act with Frank Sinatra in his Tony Rome sequel *The Lady in Cement* and turned up in the Peter Sellers/Ringo Starr farrago *The Magic Christian* (1969) playing, perhaps predictably, the Priestess of the Whip.

Welch was a pin-up and 'Playboy' sensation (the magazine labelled her "the most desired woman of the '70s", even though she never posed completely nude for them) and even hosted her own TV show. But the film she chose as her first of the '70s would prove the most divisive of her career - *Myra Breckinridge* (fortunately unavailable on DVD at the time of writing). This is one helluva mess and probably only got made because Welch's name was attached (alongside fellow sufferer Mae West, returning to the screen after a nearly 30-year absence... and

9

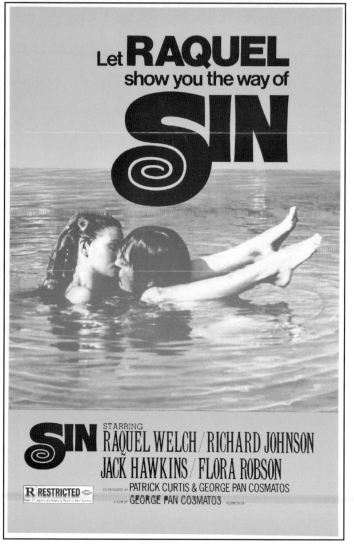

wondering why she bothered). Incompetent director Mike Sarne deserves most of the blame, though Gore Vidal should shoulder some responsibility too - his satirical novel about a transsexual who becomes a Hollywood sensation could only have been written in the '60s after a fair bit of pot smoking. *Myra Breckinridge* is considered one of the worst films ever made - justifiably, in this writer's opinion. Counter-culture classic it is not. Camp cult curio it may well be.

Her second movie of 1970, *The Beloved* (aka *Sin*), is another misfire best avoided, a tawdry romantic drama, directed in Cyprus by debut film-maker George Pan Cosmatos. See it only if you've ever wondered what Welch might look like erotically trampling grapes. In the same year, she did a superb Mae West impersonation during a Beatles' *Rocky Raccoon* skit (with Bob Hope) on her TV special *Raquel*, showing she was quite capable of sending herself up - which she did willingly, to great effect, a few years later in Richard Lester's *The Three Musketeers*.

She more than made up for *Myra* the following year, when she starred in her third western, *Hannie Caulder* (1971) which is a cracker. Directed by Burt Kennedy, a bit of a dab hand in this genre, this revenge drama has a feminist twist (which basically means it presents a woman wearing a poncho with not much else beneath it - the effect, somewhat different from Clint Eastwood turning up in

the same attire, is sure to keep the dads happy).

It would be fair to say that the '70s saw a worrying number of women getting sexually or physically assaulted on screen (Sam Peckinpah's *Straw Dogs* [1971] being the most notorious example) and *Caulder* is another which can be added to that list. After being attacked and gang-raped by brutal outlaws who are on the run following a disastrous bank robbery, Caulder (Welch, sexy and sassy, as usual) sets out on a trail

of retribution. It's possibly the first time in a western where the main protagonist is female (*Johnny Guitar* being the possible exception and, arguably, *True Grit*). She enlists the help of a bounty hunter (a bearded Robert Culp, looking a lot like Peter Fonda) to teach her to use a pistol, etc. It may be a feminist pic, but in the '70s women still needed help with the basics apparently.

Caulder is a sort of *I Spit on your Grave* prototype, filmed in Spain, with a good supporting cast. *Wild Bunchers*

Ernest Borgnine and Strother Martin (both a little too OTT) and *Once Upon a Time in the West's* Jack Elam play the repellent Clemens brothers, responsible for the assault on Hannie. As this is a British film (it was produced by Tigon - the company behind some pretty good horror films like *Witchfinder General* and *Blood on Satan's Claw*), it also has supporting roles for Christopher Lee (who would re-unite with Welch on *The Three Musketeers)* as an amicable gunmaker and a past-her-prime sexpot Diana Dors as Madame, a part similar to the character played by Rachel Roberts in *Wild Rovers* the same year.

There are several good moments in the movie. There's also a fair bit of dated ogling of Ms. Welch's assets, and the mix of crude slapstick and violence doesn't always come off ("Look what we got for supper," leers Martin on first encountering Welch's character). The interplay between Welch and Culp is well handled, the locations are used to great effect by cinematographer Edward Scaife, and Ken Thorne's score is memorable (in the tradition of *The Big Country*). Thorne had a good relationship with the director Richard Lester and his next gig was scoring his rather good 'there's-a-bomb-on-the-boat' suspenser *Juggernaut* (1974). Lester was, at the same time, working on his *Three* and *Four Musketeers* movies, though *they* ended up being scored by Michel Legrand and Lalo Schifrin, respectively.

Somewhat predictably, Quentin Tarantino has championed *Hannie Caulder,* citing it as a major influence on his *Kill Bill* movies (and maybe *The Hateful Eight)* and its legacy can definitely be found in Sam Raimi's excellent *The Quick and the Dead* (1995). *Caulder's* no masterpiece but it provided Welch with her most memorable role of the early '70s. "There are no hard women," she says at one point, "there are only soft men." The final credits ("Ernest Borgnine was… Robert Culp was…" etc. but **"Raquel Welch IS..."**) say it all.

1972 was Welch's *annus mirabilis* and she turned in two of her most enjoyable performances (but made her "other" worst film). Richard A. Colla's *Fuzz,* for which she would be paid a whacking $100,000 for nine days'

work, is a based one of Ed McBain's 89th Precinct novels (adapted by the author, under his real name Evan Hunter). Surprisingly, it co-stars Burt Reynolds. Apparently, Welch agreed to go back on her word about never working with him again but insisted they never actually properly share a scene together. When they appear to, doubles are being used.

Also featured in the excellent ensemble are Yul Brynner (who would follow this with his iconic role as The Gunslinger in Michael Crichton's *Westworld*), Jack Weston, Tom Skerritt and Dan Frazer, whom older viewers will recognise as Kojak's long-suffering boss Captain Frank McNeil (here playing an almost identical role).

It's a multi-stranded black comic cop drama, which came out in the same year as Richard Fleischer's slightly better *The New Centurions,* (the first of several '70s movies based on the brilliant books by former cop Joseph Wambaugh). The basic premise? An extortionist is tracked down by an apparently inept team of cops. The team is joined by Welch's tough-talking but sexy Detective McHenry, who is "much bigger" than expected when she first meets them, dressed in a body-hugging white jumper. Highlights include the movie poster (it shows Welch in a skimpy outfit that

HERE COME THE **"FUZZ"**

FILMWAYS presents A MARTIN RANSOHOFF Production
"FUZZ"
starring
BURT REYNOLDS JACK WESTON TOM SKERRITT
also starring **YUL BRYNNER** as"The Deaf Man"
and **RAQUEL WELCH**
Executive Producer EDWARD S. FELDMAN Screenplay by EVAN HUNTER
Based on the Novel by ED McBAIN Produced by JACK FARREN Directed by RICHARD A. COLLA
PG PARENTAL GUIDANCE SUGGESTED SOME MATERIAL MAY NOT BE SUITABLE FOR PRE-TEENAGERS Music by DAVE GRUSIN A FILMWAYS-JAVELIN Picture **United Artists** Entertainment from Transamerica Corporation

she doesn't actually wear in the film, and also depicts Reynolds recreating his infamous 'Cosmopolitan' pose… something for the ladies, presumably); some amusing moments when the cops go undercover dressed as nuns; and a tiny role for the ubiquitous weasel-faced character-actor Charles Tyner.

The nifty Isaac Hayes-esque soundtrack is by Dave Grusin, a prolific composer of the '70s, noted for his subsequent working relationships with both Warren Beatty and Sydney Pollack (he scored *The Yakuza, Three Days of the Condor, Heaven Can Wait, The Electric Horseman* and *Reds*, alongside many others).

Fuzz is most definitely ripe for re-discovery (if you can get hold of it) as is Welch's second film of the year, Jerrold Freedman's roller-skating drama *Kansas City Bomber* (expertly shot by Fred J. Koenekamp) which is

a sort of prototype *Whip It,* in which she's (wait for it) "the hottest thing on wheels."

Bomber is set in the world of women's roller derby (a hybrid mixture of wrestling, roller-skating and ice hockey) but it's one of those '70s sports films which takes the time to look at the places and faces around it (like Huston's *Fat City,* Aldrich's *The Longest Yard* and Hill's *Slap Shot*). Welch plays gum-chewin' KC Carr, a sexy and spirited single parent who finds solace and self-actualisation by beating the shit out of other women whilst on roller skates. Her main rival, Jackie Burdette, is played by wild-haired Greek actress Helena Kallianiotes, who was nominated for a Golden Globe for her supporting performance (she had previously played a small but memorable role in Bob Rafelson's *Five Easy Pieces*). Kevin McCarthy turns up as the smarmy and manipulative owner of the team with whom KC has an unlikely affair ("We're all used, that's American Pie," he pronounces) and Jodie Foster makes her debut as Rita, Welch's similarly skate lovin'

daughter. Apparently, *Bomber* is the only film she made at the time which Welch actually liked (her own company ended up producing it). The production was shut down for two months after she broke her wrist performing one of the stunts and, in many ways, the movie feels like a feminist *Rollerball* (the ironic ending is practically identical), except this one is set in the present, in Portland, Oregon. It's definitely a ride worth taking, containing arguably Welch's best movie role, albeit a bikini-free one for those doing the counting.

The turgid horror film *Bluebeard* (directed by the once-great Edward Dmytryk who, in another life, made brilliant film noirs like *Murder, My Sweet* [1944] and *Crossfire* [1947] as well as excellent war movies such as *The Caine Mutiny* [1954] and *The Young Lions* [1958]) is a strange Richard Burton vehicle in which Welch cameos (alongside several other of the world's most beautiful women played by the not-quite-in-the-same-league, Virna Lisi, Nathalie Delon, Agostina Belli, Marilu Tolo and Sybil Danning (the latter being the only one who gives Raquel a run for her money). It's probably best avoided, unless you've got a morbid interest in watching one of the greatest actors of his generation piss

of working with" (quite something coming from an actor who'd acted opposite Ava Gardner, Judy Garland, Sophia Loren and Ursula Andress). But the film has subsequently acquired a cult reputation and is definitely worth seeking out - if only for the scenes where a bikini clad Welch goes sunbathing on deck. The cast, dressed as monks for reasons too complicated to explain, run around searching for clues in a deserted monastery (a set designed by James Bond genius Ken Adam) and discover, instead, a scary Coburn dressed in drag as Welch. In the wordy but twisty finale, all is revealed to be not quite what you expected. Welch, to be honest, is given little to do here, but the

his career down the drain, or if you have a coffin fetish. Ennio Morricone wrote the better-than-the-film-deserves score, probably the only thing of interest in an otherwise muddled and plodding shambles.

Her role as a sexy but surly starlet in the whodunit *The Last of Sheila* (1973), the kind of film *Knives Out* and its sequel wished they could be, is part of that film's enduring appeal. This really is a one-off. Scripted by none other than Norman Bates himself, Anthony Perkins, along with lyricist Stephen Sondheim (yup, you read that right), and directed by former choreographer Herbert Ross (who had just worked with Woody Allen on *Play it Again, Sam* [1972]), the movie features a number of interesting '70s actors, including the charismatic James Coburn, Dyan Cannon and Richard Benjamin, as well as old-hand James Mason. The basic premise is that a bunch of movie types are holed up on a luxury yacht in the Mediterranean and are invited to play a complex parlour game which reveals their hidden secrets. Welch more-or-less plays herself, though she was led to believe her character was based on Ann-Margret.

It was apparently yet another unhappy shoot, with Mason telling the 'Chicago Tribune' Welch was "the most selfish, ill-mannered actress I've ever had the displeasure

film remains good fun. Director Ross, who went on to have several big hits in the decade (including Oscar-winning comedy *The Goodbye Girl* in 1977) holds the whole thing together with some skill, whilst Bette Midler sings the film's ironic outro *(You Got to Have) Friends*, written by the implausibly named Buzzy Linhart and Mark 'Moogy' Klingman.

I suppose it was somewhat inevitable, given Welch's stand out bosom, that someone would eventually realise the best genre to make use of her voluptuous décolletage would be the bodice-popping historical drama, and that's exactly what happened next. In 1973, she was cast (by Richard Lester) as the sexy but silly Constance Bonacieux (apparently *not* a pun, I'm reliably informed) in his massively successful and superbly mounted *The Three Musketeers* (returning for its sequel *The Four Musketeers,* the following year).

The two films were shot back-to-back to keep down costs (which caused a lot of inevitable legal wrangling between cast and producer Ilya Salkind, who had previously produced the noxious *Bluebeard* and would subsequently, with his father Alexander, go on to unleash *Superman* upon the world in 1978). Both movies feature a veritable cornucopia of '70s talent. As well as Welch, there's the glorious Faye Dunaway in a rare comic turn as Milady de Winter (although, to be fair, she *had* previously revealed her comic chops in Arthur Penn's *Little Big Man* in 1970) and Geraldine Chaplin as Anne of Austria, looking more and more like her father as she grew older. The male cast is equally splendid with the dashing Musketeers being played by Michael York, Oliver Reed, Frank Finlay and Richard Chamberlain. There are also significant roles for Charlton Heston (as the back-stabbing Cardinal Richelieu), Christopher Lee (on good form as principal baddie the one-eyed Count de Rochefort) and Simon Ward as the charming Duke of Buckingham. Stealing the show, however, are the eccentric Spike Milligan (in Part One only, unfortunately) as Welch's traitorous and horny husband; Roy Kinnear (who was also excellent in Lester's *Juggernaut*, shot around the same time) as Planchet, D'Artagnan's comic manservant; and a hilarious blink-and-you'll-miss-it cameo from Rodney Bewes. Sybil Danning, who'd had a small part in the disastrous *Bluebeard*, also appears in both films as the duplicitous Eugenie. This is a very entertaining slice of derring-do hokum, slapstick and swashbuckling thrills, with Lester's slightly surreal sense of humour never far away (although one wonders how things might have turned out had Lester

managed to cast The Beatles in the main roles as originally intended).

After a decade being widely ignored by the Awards community, Welch was finally acknowledged for her comedic talents and given a well-deserved Best Actress Golden Globe for her role as Constance and she is supremely funny throughout. The catfight between her and Dunaway needs to be seen to be believed. This laugh out loud, lavishly mounted and supremely enjoyable movie is rounded off by a forthcoming attractions trailer for *The Four Musketeers* which leaves you genuinely wanting more.

Unfortunately, *The Four Musketeers* (aka *The Revenge of Milady*), which arrived a year later, is a far less successful affair. Welch is off-screen for most of it (as is Roy Kinnear) and, apart from a priceless scene where she knowingly hides a key in her amply displayed cleavage, she makes little impression. Instead, Dunaway dominates and is highly watchable and stunningly attired throughout (by costume designer Yvonne Blake - who would go on to design Superman's outfit in 1978). It's interesting to see manic depressive actor, the pasty-faced Michael Gothard (who had appeared in Ken Russell's *The Devils*), develop his role from Part One as a devout but tormented gaoler (he'd later hang himself in 1992). Generally, this is a slightly messy and disappointing sequel, although it is infinitely better than the embarrassing Raquel-free *The Return of the Musketeers*, which Lester also directed in 1989.

Welch follows the Musketeer films with a particularly wooden turn as fading (but still sexy) glamour girl Queenie in the little seen (and heavily re-edited by its distributor) R-rated Merchant Ivory adaptation of James Moncure March's brilliant 1926 poem 'The Wild Party'.

Rewatching it for this article, I found this wannabe musical (screenwriter Walter Marks' songs are the best thing in it), which takes the infamous Fatty Arbuckle sex assault scandal of the '20s as its inspiration, a talky and slightly distasteful misfire. It was another fraught production, with Welch apparently wanting both director James Ivory *and* Academy Award winning cinematographer Walter Lassally to be fired. It's a really odd product to come from exploitation producers American International Pictures (AIP), whose prolific '70s output included stuff like *The Vampire Lovers*, *The Abominable Dr Phibes*, *Frogs*, *Scream Blacula Scream* and *Vampira*.

The original poem begins with the immortal lines "Queenie was a blonde and her age stood still. She danced twice a day in vaudeville." Unfortunately, for some reason, these are re-written for the film (which, in this reviewer's opinion is akin to re-writing T.S. Eliot) and it remains stagey and inert throughout (even the orgy scenes are tired). At least Welch finally gets to sing and dance on the big screen and, inevitably, looks good as a character whose best years are behind her but isn't going to let that stop her.

Along for the (wild) ride is the rather dislikeable James

Coco (who'd follow this with *Murder by Death* and *The Cheap Detective*) as fictional silent movie star Jolly Grimm, eager to kickstart his ailing film career by hosting the eponymous party. Also in the mix, playing Dale Sword (Grimm's rival in love), is Perry King who appeared in several notable if offbeat roles in the '70s. In the minor role of Tex, Grimm's only friend, is veteran character and comedy actor Royal Dano, who a year later would feature in Eastwood's *The Outlaw Josey Wales*. The little-known cult actress Tiffany Bolling, whose eyes remind one of Karen Black's, plays Sword's lover Kate and gets to sing (mime?) the film's comedown number (even though it's *not* a musical).

The Wild Party stands alongside John Byrum's *Inserts* (1975) and Richard Lester's *The Ritz* (1976) as one of those frank, mid-'70s X-rated (in the UK) Hollywood

films which capitalised on the new permissiveness yet failed to find much of an audience: possibly a bit too risqué for older viewers and, at the same time, too tame for the next generation of moviegoers used to a diet of post-*Texas Chainsaw Massacre* horror and *Deep Throat* sex.

In 1976, Welch played Jugs (finally, a film that manages to work its main selling point into Welch's character's nickname *and* the movie's title) in Peter Yates' unpopular and not especially funny black comedy *Mother, Jugs and Speed*. The film was covered in detail by John Harrison in 'Cinema of the '70s' Issue 7. Whilst certainly not Yates' best film of the '70s (that would be *The Friends of Eddie Coyle*), it's not bad. That said, many of its attitudes are woefully of their time. Bill Cosby's presence may also put off modern viewers, but it's fun to watch Harvey Keitel (hot off *Taxi Driver*) tap into his comedic side for once, and

to see '70s stalwarts Allen Garfield, Bruce Davison, Larry Hagman and renowned western actor LQ Jones in minor roles.

The following year, Welch had a cameo as Lady Edith in Richard Fleischer's *The Prince and the Pauper* (aka *Crossed Swords*), another bodice ripper which re-united several stars (Heston, Reed and Sybil Danning) with the producers and writer (George MacDonald Fraser) of the Musketeers films but to significantly less effect. The added wattage of

George C. Scott, Rex Harrison, Ernest Borgnine, David Hemmings and Mark Lester isn't enough to bring it up to the level of the earlier pics.

Her final movie of the '70s was Claude Zidi's *L'Animal* (aka *Stuntwoman*) (1977), a French action comedy in which she appeared alongside Gallic superstar Jean Paul Belmondo. The less said about it, the better. It marks a major downturn in her popularity - although, to be fair, none of her post-*Musketeers* films had shown much box office clout.

1978 did see Welch give one of her most memorable performances, as a special guest in the third season of TV's *The Muppet Show*, where she sings and dances with Fozzie Bear, a weird spider puppet and, most memorably, Miss Piggy, duetting with her on a very funny *I'm a Woman* ("W.O.... P.I.G," they sing together).

However, the times, as the man said, were a changin'. Punk had blown apart the music scene but its effects on other aspects of popular culture throughout the world were far-reaching. Perhaps Welch was suddenly a bit old-fashioned or, possibly, the more inclusive attitude towards gender fostered by the punks made her an object of scorn rather than lust? Maybe soft-core smut like 1974's *Emmanuelle* (and its numerous sequels), David Hamilton's soft focus *Bilitis* (1977) and, in the UK at least, the endless tide of sex comedies like *Confessions of a Window Cleaner*, *Adventures of a Plumber's Mate* and *The Ups and Downs of a Handyman* et al, with their full frontal nudity and frank representations of sex acts, had rendered a chaste performer like Welch (who had never even gone topless) somehow redundant? In 1979, after all, Blake Edwards made a big star of Bo Derek on the basis of her willingness to show off her breasts in his huge smash *10*. Even Edwards' wife - the previously demure Julie Andrews, no less - was persuaded to bare all in his next movie, the

satirical comedy *SOB* (1981) and she went on to play a cross-dresser a year later in *Victor/Victoria*.

In addition, at the tail end of the '70s, the video industry had finally ushered in a new era of pornography in the form of above (and below) the counter adult home entertainment. This probably played its part in desensitising viewers when it came to sex and sexuality on screen. Why would anyone use their imagination when they could now literally watch hours of the real thing and then press rewind to consume it all over again?

Welch withdrew from movies and set herself up as a rather good cabaret performer, often singing and dancing to the new disco rhythms that were dominating contemporary airwaves. She became the manager of a huge (what else?) beauty empire, specialising in fitness videos and wigs. She endured a massive legal battle with MGM in 1982, when they accused her of being unprofessional after she pulled out of her planned comeback film *Cannery Row*. She won the case with the aid, surprisingly, of Burt Reynolds who noted in his autobiography "she thanked me for my help, but we still don't send Christmas cards." The whole affair made her *persona non grata* in Hollywood, and she subsequently spent the latter part of her career on TV, with the odd cameo thrown in (1994's *Naked Gun 33 and 1/3*, for example).

Of course, there have been leagues of attractive American actresses since Welch, but none have come close to being perceived as the physical embodiment of hetero-normative desire in female form, which is what happened to Welch. She famously quipped: "I was not

brought up to be a sex symbol... the fact that I became one is probably the loveliest, most glamorous and fortunate misunderstanding."

Raquel Welch was the last of the bombshells. She was - hem, hem - built to last!

(This article is dedicated to my father, who used to tell me there were always two good reasons to see a new Raquel Welch film. He wasn't wrong. He rarely was).

THE HARDER THEY COME

JIMMY CLIFF in

Don't... Fuck... Wid... Me! by Ian Talbot Taylor

"Don't... fuck... wid... me!" Sound advice, delivered by the main character in Jamaica's very first feature film. Other advice delivered by another character is somewhat less abrasive: "Sit tight and listen keenly"...so says the DJ at the dance in Perry Henzell's iconic Kingston-based drama *The Harder They Come*, a combination of music, crime, tragedy and realistic presentation of life for many of the poorer inhabitants of Jamaica during the early '70s. Fittingly, the character is played by none other than Prince Buster, the 'Voice of the People', a DJ and performer of Ska, the forefather of the slowed down form - Reggae - that would eventually reach out and embrace the world.

Indeed, some would have it that *The Harder They Come* was responsible for 'bringing Reggae to the world', but it would be more accurate to say that it raised awareness in the USA. In actual fact, *Israelites* by Desmond Dekker and the Aces had reached number one in the UK on April 16, 1969, becoming the first to do so. The record also fared well (though not *as* well) Stateside. Reggae owed its roots to Mento, a Jamaican folk music that emerged in the 1940s/'50s. The popularity of this began to fade in the '60s, when Jamaican radios began to pick up US stations playing Rhythm & Blues. The combination of traditional island music/general culture and these American influences helped to create a distinctive new sound that became prolific in Jamaica, and also spread to the UK (no doubt helped by post-war migration). Reggae hits were occurring as early as 1964.

Nevertheless, Henzell's movie raised awareness to another level. It didn't just shine a realistic light on Jamaican life, it also provided the country with its very own cinematic success.

Perry Henzell started off working on adverts, and even worked for the BBC. Beverley Anderson (now Beverley Manley) who played the role of a wealthy and disparaging housewife in the film and later married Michael Manley (who became the Prime Minister of Jamaica), observed that Henzell "had this dream, he had this wish to do a movie that was going to be a success."

The use of music was an obvious choice. Chris Blackwell, the man behind the legendary Island Records, has noted the "tremendous amount of creativity in the music field. A lot of records being made." Surely, the public would pay to watch a combination of the western outlaws that they lapped up at cinemas like the Rialto and the Ska/Reggae sounds that they danced to?

Henzell sought authenticity and turned to a leading man who had lived the life of a young man coming to the city to try and make a record. He saw the man that he wanted on the sleeve of a hit record. On the front cover, the man was photographed face on and was young, good-looking, almost angelic. On the flipside, however, his profile shot made him look "like a sufferer!" Henzell was sure that anyone who could change his persona just by being captured at a different angle or using a different expression would be perfect. Unfortunately, the singer was under contract to Island Records, leading to negotiations with Blackwell that would free the performer up. And who was this sought after singer?

Popular Reggae star Jimmy Cliff (UK Top 50 single *Vietnam* (1969) and Top 10 singles *Wonderful World, Beautiful People* (1969) and *Wild World* (1970), in the US *Wonderful World...* would make the top 30 and its follow-up *Come into My Life* edged into 89th slot) plays Ivanhoe Martin, who was inspired by a genuine Jamaican criminal of the same name better known as Rhyging. The original script was actually entitled *Rhygin* and then *Ivan*. He was a real-life 'rude boy', a slang term that came from the poorer sections of Kingston, Jamaica, and was associated with discontented youths prone to robbery and violence.

They listened to Ska and rocksteady (a slower version of Ska, usually replacing trombone with piano and stronger bass, and offering more socially and politically conscious lyrics) music, and tended to wear sharp suits, thin ties and pork pie or trilby hats, clearly influenced by the fashions of US jazz and soul musicians who had achieved infamy during the '40s and became something of an urban legend.

Cliff's interpretation of 'Ivan' Martin clearly follows in the footsteps of the original and is presented as a poor Jamaican man who leaves the countryside for Kingston Town, in desperate search of work. Henzell wanted to cast people who would know more about their characters than he himself did. Cliff was perfect. Almost immediately he has all his possessions robbed and despite his excitement with city life (such as the music and the bustling trips to a run-down cinema where the locals lap up the famous spaghetti western *Django)*, he fails to find any worthwhile job.

The script, written by Henzell and Trevor D. Rhone, offers us a Caribbean flavoured kitchen sink drama as Ivan finds himself involved with, and let down by, a succession of people and communities. His wastrel mother is revealed to be a poor role model from the start, and he inadvertently comes under the watchful eye a Christian preacher and his foreman, both of whom treat him to both verbal and physical harshness. Ivan provokes the preacher's ire due to his showing amorous interest in the preacher's virginal young ward Elsa and is then thrown out of the circle for using the church to rehearse non-religious songs.

Henzell had first met Rhone at The Barn Theatre and he immediately asked him to write his film script. The writer confessed that he had no experience nor the urge to try, but Henzell was persuasive. The rawness of Rhone's work helped achieve just what Henzell wanted. And anyway, the script was often pretty much set aside according to Winston Stona who played the moderately corrupt Detective Ray Jones.

As the tale unfolds, delivered in full-on Jamaican dialect, so much so that many releases of the picture required English language subtitles, the gritty and bleak tale set amongst the shanty towns of the city is so convincing it almost feels like a documentary.

The continuing script sees the preacher's lackey try to steal from Ivan the bicycle that he has spent time and money repairing and this is the straw that breaks the camel's back. Ivan challenges the bigger man to a fight and, dodging the broken bottle the other man uses against him, Ivan slashes him with a knife, punctuating his attack with the warning: "Don't... fuck... wid... me!" Whilst Ivan retains his bicycle and develops something of a formidable reputation, he is sentenced to a vicious and demeaning whipping by the local authorities. This is a brutal scene indeed, and demeaning in the extreme. Henzell doesn't shy away from the pain, nor the indignity as Ivan's bladder gives in during the punishment (getting the lash as he has a slash!) and he clearly urinates before a solemn audience.

This is a pivotal moment. Ivan might be pretty lazy and reckless to the point of naivety in the way he frustrates the authority figures around him, but he has at least been trying to earn an honest living. In Henzell and Rhone's script, our (anti) hero not only responds by defiantly reaching for the stars, but he also shuns the straight and

narrow. Even more crucially, his cruel punishment and embarrassment emotionally scar him enough to cause serious, and eventually fatal, consequences.

Before he hits rock bottom, however, Ivan makes an attempt at becoming a Reggae singing star. He approaches a prominent record producer with a song that he has written and delivers a scorching version of it in the studio. This was *The Harder They Come*, a track written and recorded for real by Jimmy Cliff, and the one that convinced the director to retitle the entire movie.

In 1986, Cliff was interviewed about the film and talked about his casting, inspired by that old record sleeve. It was, he said "the trend of his career", balancing the angelic and the dangerous. "They are both valid to my public." It is true that before *The Harder They Come* was released, the singer was best known for the upbeat and positive Pop Reggae track *Wonderful World, Beautiful People*. Cliff still felt that the juxtaposition of the two sides to his personality were key to his success, though he wished to promote the "hope of love". What was sacred to him? "Truth and life".

Those contrasting elements of darkness and light can also be witnessed in the balancing of sublime music and harsh visuals. It would have been easy for Henzell to present a gorgeous looking travelogue, but he opted for honesty. The opening shot of the landscape might be of the ocean and the coastline, but the weather is harsh, windy and grey. The beach holiday beauty is cast aside in favour of tin shacks, dodgy clubs and marijuana fields. This plays out though, before a soundtrack of Jamaican music at its best. The scenes of Cliff performing *The Harder They Come* and Toots and the Maytals performing *Pressure Drop* are massive highlights, whilst other quality artists such as The Slickers, The Melodians and Scotty also feature.

Now, in many a musical drama, the principal character would slowly but surely climb the ladder to fame and fortune, but this wasn't the story that Henzell wanted to deliver. Instead, he opted for a realistic exposé of the music industry in Jamaica at the time. Big-shot producers with their studios, sound systems and record stores could monopolise the entire movement and make the bulk of the money as poor young men and women would record for a pittance. The plot of the movie sees Ivan earn a standard exploitative offer of $20. His song becomes a huge hit, but it is the producer who benefits.

Desperate, Ivan begins to move marijuana the drug from the countryside to the city via motorbike. Unknown to Ivan, this is part of a police-protected network. Unfortunately, when he complains about the poor pay (yet again!) he is set up by his friend/boss José. Ivan is flagged down by a policeman and, haunted by his previous humiliating whipping at the hands of the authorities, Ivan panics and shoots the policeman dead.

Later, the police attempt to capture him, but Ivan shoots his way out, killing three officers. Now, he is on the run, even as his hit record blares from the island's radio speakers. The record producer is capitalising on Ivan's new infamy. The finale of the film echoes that early screening of *Django* as Ivan is cornered on a beach by automatic rifle-bearing policemen. He demands they send out their baddest man. We might remember José's earlier comment about *Django* - "Him think the hero can die till the last real!"

The '60s spaghetti westerns had really become popular in Jamaica, as can be inferred by such musical recordings as *Return of Django* by The Upsetters, *Jesse James* by Laurel Aitken and even a reworking of the theme from *The Guns of Navarone* by Freddie Notes & the Rudies that saw the lead singer toasting about killing Clint Eastwood! One can only hope that he meant the Man with No Name character and not the actual actor! The early scene in the ramshackle cinema highlights this working-class obsession with cinematic outlaws, whilst the finale of the film shows how the lack of fair opportunities drove the young men to fantasy-fuelled crime sprees as the rude boys proliferated.

Henzell recalled that *The Harder They Come* "was the spirit of the city seen through the eyes of a country boy". Transistor radios were becoming popular, so small farmers and youngsters were getting news and sounds from the city and were being drawn there for success. It was an illusion. Like so many, Ivan would "rather lose his life than give up on the dream."

Trevor Rhone remembers that nobody was in it for the money - "it was an act of faith", and that faith paid off. The film was a hit in Jamaica because of the naturalistic representation of black Jamaicans using their real voices in genuine locations. "Black people seeing themselves on the screen for the first time created an unbelievable audience reaction," said Henzell.

After a premiere in Kingston on June 5, 1972, it was released in February 1973 in New York City by Roger Corman's New World. At first its wider appeal was slight, but that soundtrack really did boost the music and culture of Jamaica, and the movie slowly but surely grew into a cult classic. Ivan became the tragic hero who died trying to claim "the pie up in the sky, waiting for me when I die" ahead of his fate.

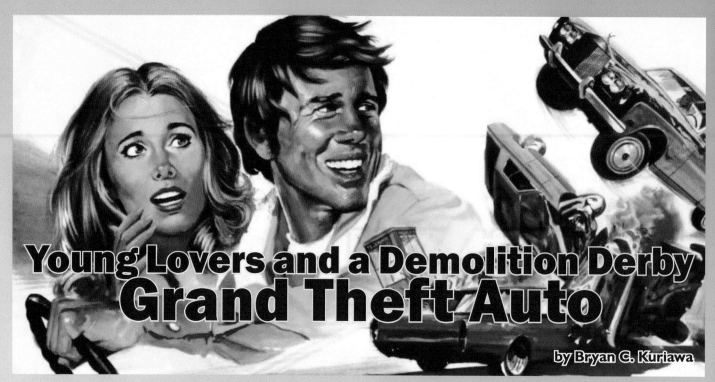

Young Lovers and a Demolition Derby
Grand Theft Auto

by Bryan C. Kuriawa

By the late '70s, the era of the B-movie was coming to an end. American International Pictures (AIP) was transitioning to A-list productions with films like *The Island of Dr. Moreau* (1977) and *Meteor* (1979). Other companies like Crown International Pictures and Allied Artists began shutting down and selling off their existing library to bigger studios. Despite being poised against the establishment, New Hollywood had consolidated the position of the major studios to a great extent.

At New World Pictures, Roger Corman continued his reign as the king of B-movies. After his success at AIP in the years prior, he wanted a little more control.

Working within the same parameters as his previous works, he produced a string of cult box-office hits including *Death Race 2000*, *TNT Jackson* (both 1975), *Piranha* (1978) and *Rock and Roll High School* (1979) among others. He also imported multiple foreign films including Federico Fellini's *Amarcord*, Shiro Moritani's *Submersion of Japan* (both 1973) and *Lone Wolf and Cub: Baby Cart at The River Styx* (1972). The latter two would be re-edited and distributed in the United States in new versions called, respectively, *Tidal Wave* (1975) and *Shogun Assassin* (1980).

Much like his time at AIP and Filmgroup, Corman continued to bring new directors, writers, actors and other personnel up through the ranks. In 1977, he'd start a familiar TV actor on the path to becoming a very successful future filmmaker. The only question: "How many cars to wreck?"

"You Know How Reckless These Young People Can Be"

In Beverly Hills, Sam Freeman (Ron Howard) and his girlfriend, Paula Powers (Nancy Morgan) arrive at Paula's parents' house. They've come to ask her parents for their blessing to get married. Paula's father, business magnate Bigby Powers (Barry Cahill), rejects this entirely. With his future plans to be governor, Bigby wants Paula to marry Collins Hedgeworth (Paul Linke), the heir to the Hedgeworth fortune.

Sam is kicked out and Paula sent to her room, but the two lovebirds are undeterred. Paula sneaks out and steals her father's Rolls Royce. Their goal: make it to Las Vegas and elope. Angered by his daughter's insolence, Bigby turns to a private investigator (Rance Howard) and his team to try to thwart their efforts.

Learning of his supposed fiancée's plans, Collins races after Paula, hoping he can change her mind. Wrecking his car and borrowing another from a local dealership, he's on his way, yet not before he calls into the radio show of local DJ Curly Q. Brown (Don Steele) and offers $25,000 for Paula's return. Panicked by her son's behavior, Collins' mother Vivian (Marion Ross) also calls Brown's show offering $25,000 for her son's return.

With multiple factions chasing after them - including two disturbed auto mechanics, an overzealous preacher, a frustrated Los Angeles cop and the P.I. team among others, all while Brown broadcasts from a helicopter above - Sam and Paul have a lot to contend with.

Shot in four weeks on a budget of $602,000, *Grand Theft Auto* is a fun directorial debut for Ron Howard. An over-the-top comedy, it encapsulates the great thrill of a B-movie with enjoyable characters, engaging performances and, of course, vehicle mayhem.

"Wanna Pull Over and Fool Around a Little?"

Ron Howard was a symbol of postwar America to a

great degree. His father Rance had appeared in numerous films and TV shows, while his brother Clint had become a cult actor with far too many appearances in films and shows to keep track of. As for Ron, he was a figure of the TV revolution. For eight years, he'd portrayed Sheriff Andy Taylor's son on *The Andy Griffith Show* and would later be a '50s teenager on *Happy Days* for eight seasons.

During this same period, Howard also appeared in several feature films. These included *The Wild Country* (1970), *American Graffiti* (1973) and John Wayne's final movie *The Shootist* (1976). In 1976, Howard was cast in the New World Production, *Eat My Dust!* directed by Charles B. Griffith. This film starred him as a local sheriff's son who steals a stock car and faces off against his in-pursuit father. It was a modest box office hit, and Corman gave Howard a smaller salary and percentage of the film's profits. According to Corman, Howard said he would do the follow-up for free if Corman offered him the director's chair.

Given the opportunity to helm his own anarchistic auto epic, Howard had Corman's blessing. Now he had to show what he was capable of.

"Well, I Guess I Got My Head Up My Rectum Again"

Led by Howard as Sam, an interesting cast of newcomers and character actors headline this production.

Howard's Sam is a likeable guy. We don't learn too much about him, except that he doesn't want to come across like he's after Paula's family fortune. He's committed to getting married and doesn't want any complications.

As the driver and rebellious bride, Morgan's Paula is very engaging and charming. Like Sam, she's just as determined to get married, yet she views this as a revolt against her father's authority. This leads to an excellent scene, the film's only serious dramatic moment, where Sam and Paula argue in a junkyard.

Surrounded by rusty scrap metal and other junk, the two are faced with the dilemma of what they're doing and wonder if they're really ready. To paraphrase a late French author, they realize their love needs to be planned beyond this day in the sun. It's a striking moment and one of the best parts of the film.

Appearing in multiple '70s TV shows, including *McMillian and Wife*, *Lucas Tanner* and *Medical Center*, Morgan's career never really took off. Outside of an early '90s spaghetti western *Lucky Luke* (1991) starring Terence Hill, she had few standout roles. She's better remembered as the late John Ritter's wife, with whom she starred in his 1979 film *Americanthon*.

Portraying those in pursuit, the great cast includes Marion Ross, Hoke Howell, Clint and Rance Howard, Peter Isacksen, Jim Ritz and more. Trading in her '50s housewife role on *Happy Days* for an unbalanced, well-to-do woman, Ross has a lot of fun with her part. Her scenes with Ritz's cop are a great introduction to both their characters.

To be honest, it's hard to find a poor performance. Everyone from Cahill's Bigby Powers and Linke's Collins Hedgeworth, to smaller parts like Ritz's cop and the P.I team, give strong, enthusiastic performances. Real-life disc jockey Don Steele as Curly Q. Brown is a particular standout. Much like his characters in *Death Race 2000* and *Rock and Roll High School*, he turns the role of a disc jockey into an implicit media criticism. Initially sympathetic to Sam and Paula's plight, he begins following them in a helicopter and broadcasting their whereabouts. When Sam confronts Curly over Bigby's car phone, he says off-air that this is for ratings no matter what Sam says. Yet Brown does get his own comeuppance in the final scene.

"Ladies and Gentlemen, I'm Passing Through a Beautiful Suburban Home"

On a budget just under $1 million, Howard showcases how he'd learned much from being on film and TV sets in the prior two decades.

His direction is excellent and being on the road for much of the film creates a very kinetic experience. We feel like we're in a race, as the various individuals and factions literally collide. The driving sequences are well staged, moving from Los Angeles through the open California desert to a stock car demolition derby on the outskirts of Las Vegas.

Many of the desert sequences benefit from the excellent cinematography of Gary Graver. Most well remembered for his work with Orson Welles on *F for Fake* (1973) and the posthumously released *The Other Side of the Wind* (2018), Graver had a truly eclectic Hollywood career. *Grand Theft Auto* occupies a place amid the exploitation fare he lensed, which also included Al Adamson's *Dracula vs Frankenstein* (1971), *The Toolbox Murders* (1978) and several films with Fred Olan Rey, including *Alienator* (1989) and *Bikini Airways* (2003). It's also worth mentioning that Graver was the director of photography on numerous soft erotic films and, under a pseudonym, directed tons of adult titles in the '80s and '90s. Going from working with Orson Welles and Ron Howard to making the like of *Sexual Roulette* (1997) and *Diary of Lust* (2000) is quite a resumé!

Script-wise, the screenplay by Ron and his father Rance is delightful. This isn't a dramatic epic with social commentary or some modern-day over-simplistic moralizing. It's a fun ride with two young lovers trying to live their lives on their terms. To a great extent, the film is almost a companion piece to Stanley Kramer's 1963 comedy epic *It's a Mad, Mad, Mad, Mad World*. Both have a grand chase to a final location, with the wacky comedic characters and their antics filling the narrative.

The dialogue is quotable and, as indicated before, the dramatics are left to the one junkyard scene. If there is a message, it's about the trials of youth and young love. The scene of Bigby's Rolls Royce being destroyed in the demolition car rally symbolizes Sam and Paula's break with their past.

Last but not least, the soundtrack by Peter Ivers is very enjoyable. The victim of an unsolved murder in 1983, Ivers delivers an energetic score with many great cues. The signature motifs are cues set around the film's title song, sung and written by Ron Howard. It's a great accompaniment to the on-screen mayhem and it's a shame Ivers had such a short career.

"*Grand Theft Auto is a Love Story with Cars*"

Released in June 1977, the film was a box office success, grossing $15 million. Critics were largely indifferent or negative, yet, as Corman often said, all that really counts is the box office.

The film was released around the world under multiple titles. Among the more interesting were Italy's *Watch Out for That Crazy Rolls Royce*, Greece's *Crazy Car Chase* and Japan's *Vanishing in Turbo*. Incidentally, my decision to seek out the film came about after seeing a YouTube video of it being presented on Japanese TV in the '80s by actor Tadao Takashima of *King Kong vs Godzilla* (1962) fame.

In the years after its release, the film found its way to the emerging home video market. Corman's subsequent company New Concorde released it on laserdisc in the '90s and again on DVD for its 25th anniversary in 2002, then once more in 2006.

Around 2010, Shout! Factory picked up much of the New World library and released these films to DVD and Blu-ray under the banner 'Roger Corman's Cult Classics'. Both *Grand Theft Auto* and its companion film *Eat My Dust!* were released on a double feature DVD. Unfortunately, it's since gone out of print, though *Dust!* was re-released on a limited-edition Blu-ray with the 1976 film *The Great Texas Dynamite Chase*.

While the movie hasn't been referenced frequently in American pop culture, it might have an unlikely fan in TV creator Seth MacFarlane.

For the 100th episode of his animated sitcom, *American Dad!* in 2010, he crafted a plot surprisingly similar to *Grand Theft Auto*. In the show *100 A.D.*, Stan Smith (MacFarlane) has to stop his hippie daughter Hayley (Rachel MacFarlane) and her slacker boyfriend Jeff (Jeff Fischer) from eloping. When he discovers they're hiding in a massive mountain range, he calls into the local TV station and offers $50,000 for anyone who can stop the wedding. As a result, every major and one-off character chases after the couple. Whether he was paying tribute to the film, or it was a

RON HOWARD'S FUNNIER AND FASTER HE'S A HIGH SPEED DISASTER!

GRAND THEFT AUTO

See the greatest cars in the world destroyed: Rolls Royce, Cadillac, Lincoln, Mercedes, Porsche and 43 Screaming Street Machines!

RON HOWARD in 'GRAND THEFT AUTO' starring NANCY MORGAN · MARION ROSS · PETER ISACKSEN · DON STEELE · CLINT HOWARD
executive producer ROGER CORMAN   produced by JON DAVISON   written by RANCE HOWARD and RON HOWARD   directed by RON HOWARD
A NEW WORLD PICTURE   METROCOLOR

coincidence, I'll leave up to the reader.

As for Ron Howard, he proved himself and wanted to go down the path of being a full-time filmmaker. Following *Grand Theft Auto*, he directed several TV movies including 1978's *Cotton Candy* among others. With the success of 1982's *Night Shift*, his directorial career took off with such successes as *Splash* (1984), *Cocoon* (1985), *Gung Ho* (1986), *Apollo 13* (1995), *Cinderella Man* (2005), *Frost/Nixon* (2008) and more.

In Howard's subsequent career, *Grand Theft Auto* is often viewed as a footnote. Yet it's far from that and is, in fact, an overlooked gem. Howard infused the final production with a fun, delightful, adventurous spirit that takes you on a great ride. The comedic energy he brings to this production can be seen in some of his later works as well.

An out-of-control series of car wrecks was the start of a long career for one of Hollywood's most acclaimed filmmakers. In the case of Ron Howard, Corman's past success in bringing new actors and directors to the forefront paid more dividends than he could have ever imagined.

by Peter Sawford

Some serial killers are famous for their nicknames: The Boston Strangler, Son of Sam and Jack the Ripper to name just three. But one killer is so identified with an address that the address itself is every bit as infamous as its former resident, John Reginald Halliday Christie. Christie lived at 10 Rillington Place from 1937 to 1953 and, during that time, killed 8 people (including his wife). Before his arrest and execution in 1953, he played a huge role in one of the worst miscarriages of justice in British judicial history.

Based on the book 'Ten Rillington Place' by Ludovic Kennedy, and working from an excellent script by Clive Exton, the film opens in 1944 and shows Christie (Richard Attenborough) carrying out one of his earliest murders while living at the eponymous address with his wife Ethel (Pat Heywood). Thereafter, the film primarily concerns itself with the period that Timothy Evans (John Hurt) and his wife Beryl (Judy Geeson) lived at the address and Evans' subsequent trial for murder.

Throughout the '60s, producers had tried to bring the story of Christie and the crimes he committed to the big screen. They had failed, not only because the story was still considered too distressing, but because there was a law in the UK which decreed that a film couldn't be made about a real-life killer until 50 years had passed since his or her crimes. Eventually, in 1970, thanks to an Act of Parliament repealing the law, producers Leslie Linder and Martin Ransohoff were given the go-ahead to make their film version of the events. By May, production had started.

The start of filming also came at a time of seismic change in British law and order, as capital punishment had been removed from the statute books in December 1969 and was still a hot topic of debate over its relative merits. Indeed, one of the main reasons Richard Attenborough gave for appearing in the film was to highlight his abhorrence of capital punishment. He hoped the film would convince even the hardest sceptic or most ardent supporter of hanging that abolishing the death penalty was the right way to go.

One thing that worked in the producer's favour was that Rillington Place, despite being scheduled for demolition, still existed when filming began. Director Richard Fleischer, whose previous credits included *Compulsion* (1959) and *The Boston Strangler* (1968), was given full access to film in the street. While most scenes were filmed outside or close to no. 7, permission was granted - after much pleading - for him to film inside no. 10, albeit for just one shot.

Notting Hill was one of the most run down and underfunded boroughs of London in the '40s and '50s and not much had changed by the time the cameras started rolling. The exteriors still resembled what the address would have looked like at the time Christie lived there. The interiors, however, were recreated at Shepperton Studios, and Art Director Maurice Carter and Set Decorator Andrew Campbell deserving huge credit for their work. The peeling wallpaper hints at the damp creeping up the walls, and you can almost feel the squalor in the bare wooden floorboards and threadbare carpet on the stairs. The house is shabby, unloved and unkempt, mirroring the decaying state of the Christie marriage. There is no colour, no brightness, in the building; just a mass of drab browns and greys. The sunlight struggling to battle through the grimy windows and filthy net curtains creates an almost oppressive feeling of gloom. The small back yard, with its single outhouse and general clutter, offers no escape from the unpleasant surroundings. Moreover, it is the last resting place for many of Christie's unfortunate victims.

Cinematographer Denys Coop adds to the stifling sense of claustrophobia within the house. His camera is rarely more than a few feet from any given character, and the low lighting helps create a miserable atmosphere in the increasingly miserable house. Central to, and the main cause of, all the unhappiness is Attenborough's harrowing performance as Christie. Born in Cambridge in 1923, Attenborough had made his first screen appearance in Noel Coward's *In Which We Serve* (1942) and, over the following years, had appeared in films both serious (*Brighton Rock* [1948] and *The Angry Silence* [1960]) and comedic (*Private's Progress* [1956] and *I'm Alright Jack* [1959]). Perhaps his most famous role had been Sqn. Ldr Roger Bartlett, the doomed but brilliant brains behind *The Great Escape* (1963). Only the year before filming began

on *10 Rillington Place*, Attenborough had swapped to the other side of the camera and made his directorial debut with his big screen adaptation of Joan Littlewoods antiwar play *Oh! What a Lovely War* (1969).

Attenborough hadn't been the first choice for the role. Donald Pleasence was initially offered the part, but after playing Dr Crippen in the early '60s, he didn't want to become typecast as a screen murderer. Initially Attenborough was also somewhat reluctant to play Christie but turns out to be an excellent second choice, wonderfully evil as the killer. Balding, rotund and bespectacled, his voice never reaching above a whisper,

Attenborough is a constant malevolent spirit around the house, endlessly poking his nose in, peering around half-opened doors and continually appearing from out of nowhere to hear a slip of the tongue or minor indiscretion that he can use for own purposes later.

Attenborough's performance as Christie is a masterclass in 'less is more'. Always an underrated actor, he is capable of conveying more menace through a look or an extended silence than most actors can with a snarl, a punch or a knife.

Before going upstairs to "see to" Beryl, Attenborough stares long and hard at himself in the medical cabinet mirror like the enormity of what he's about to do is weighing so heavily on his conscience that he may be unable to go through with it. Moments later, once his wife has been sent out, the urge to kill overrides everything else and the tools of murder are retrieved. Armed with an ever-present cup of tea, Attenborough climbs the stairs and Beryl's fate is sealed.

Against Attenborough's strong performance, a lesser supporting actor could have disappeared into the background. In John Hurt, who plays the illiterate, uneducated Evans, himself trapped in the web spun by Christie and destined to pay the ultimate price, the producers made an inspired choice. Hurt had been acting since 1962 and made his breakthrough as Richard Rich in Fred Zinnemann's *A Man for all Seasons* (1966) but, despite appearing in that multi-Oscar-winning film, his career hadn't taken off in quite the way he'd hoped. In *10 Rillington Place*, Hurt makes Evans a sympathetic character who is not without flaws. He likes a drink for one, and this reduces his already-short fuse, leading to shouting matches and raised fists. Evans is a boy in a man's body, a fantasist to whom

31

lying comes naturally. He has no regard about whether anyone finds his stories believable or not. One minute he's telling Christie they've moved from a well-to-do area and a fine house, the next he claims that, despite his illiteracy, he's going to be promoted to the board of directors and have secretaries to do all his reading for him. Hurt conveys a wonderful sense of bewilderment; he never seems on top of any situation or totally in command of the facts. That Evans loved his wife and undoubtably his daughter is never in doubt. Fleischer's direction, Exton's script and Hurt's performance never cast the slightest doubt as to his possible guilt.

The scenes between Attenborough and Hurt are superb, with Christie tying Evans up in legal mumbo-jumbo and nonsensical renting regulations. When armed with only a basic St John's Ambulance first aid handbook, he convinces the gullible and naïve Evans that he's a medical man able to perform the abortion both Tim and Beryl feel is the only way out of their situation. While Attenborough is all calm rationality, Hurt is brilliant as the sweaty, nervous Evans, unable to properly understand either the medical or legal implications of what Christie is saying and unable to see the tragic path he's walking down. Hurt's final scene as he's led from his cell to execution still shocks to this day. A hood is pulled down over his confused, scared face and, with a crash, we're left looking at a length of taut rope, our imagination filling in the blanks.

In an unusual postscript to this scene, Albert Pierrepoint had been employed by the producers as a technical advisor. Pierrepoint was the chief executioner for the British Government until 1956 and had overseen the hanging of both Timothy Evans and John Christie. He thus found himself in the unique position of being able to critique first-hand the performance of Edwin Brown who was playing him in the film!

Against two such powerful leads it would be easy for Pat Heywood and Judy Geeson to get lost, but it's a testament to the strength of their performances that they don't.

Heywood plays Ethel Christie, a loyal wife in an unhappy, loveless marriage. Her reaction to the death of Beryl suggests she knows more than she lets on to neighbours or the police about her husband. Her quick acceptance to either hold or look after baby Geraldine are poignant indicators of the regret she feels about her childless marriage. We know her days are numbered when she threatens to leave for good and suggests to her husband that he should probably be in prison. Christie goes to the kitchen, unlocks the medical cabinet, and shortly afterwards we see him ominously replacing floorboards in the living room.

Judy Geeson depicts Beryl as an essentially good person in a marriage made unhappy by poverty. She loves her husband but hates their circumstances and living conditions. Like him, she is unable to see though Christie's lies to save herself and daughter. Beryl constantly tries to make the best of a horrible existence. There's evidence of a potential warmth, a friendship even, with Ethel, but it's Christie's obvious infatuation with her that seals her fate.

For a film made so soon after the actual crimes, *10 Rillington Place* doesn't flinch in showing how Christie's victims met their fates. Although the death of Ethel is subtly implied, Fleischer doesn't downplay the true horror of what Christie was doing. The first murder is shown in some detail, but the killing of Beryl is stretched out to an agonising six minutes with Christie quietly, always quietly, explaining what he's going to do while Beryl, trusting and innocent, makes his task easy. Too late, she realises what's

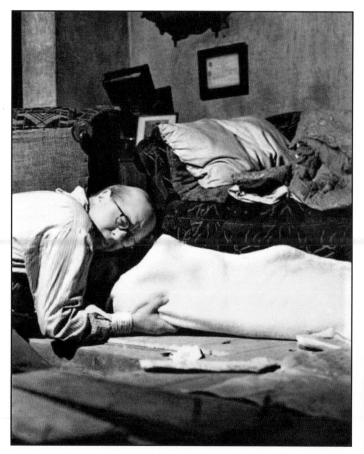

32

actually happening, and Christie is forced to switch to a more violent approach. It's quite traumatising to realise these events actually happened. A young life such as Beryl's was violently snuffed out in real life; this isn't just some fevered imaginary serial killer melodrama that seeks to shock and scare.

Eventually, his life empty, shunned by the neighbours and no longer willing to live with the bodies scattered around the property, Christie leaves and lives for a while as a vagrant. He is eventually recognised by a uniformed PC and arrested and taken into custody. The film ends on a freeze frame of Christies face, with two title cards explaining Christie was hanged at Pentonville Prison and that, twelve years later, Evans was pardoned and re-buried in consecrated grounds.

Although Attenborough, Hurt, Heywood and Geeson share the majority of screen time, a fine cast is rounded out by Isobel Black as Beryl's friend Alice who almost stumbles across Christie in the act of killing her friend. In the courtroom at Evan's trial, Robert Hardy plays defence lawyer Malcolm Morris, given the hopeless task of saving Evans from the rope, while Geoffrey Chater plays Prosecutor Christmas Humphreys, attempting to do the complete opposite. Andre Morrell, playing Judge Lewis, displays an air of complete indifference towards Evan's plight.

Apart from the mournful, almost morose music over the opening titles, the music by John Dankworth is hardly used. Fleischer allows the story to tell itself without the need for music to heighten the scenes.

At the 1971 BAFTA's John Hurt was nominated for Best Supporting Actor but lost out to Edward Fox for *The Go-Between* while Attenborough was totally overlooked for Best Actor. Even today, *10 Rillington Place* retains the power to shock and initiate debate about capital punishment. Even the most ardent supporter of the death penalty will find it difficult to answer the questions the film poses.

During the '80s, whenever the possible resumption of capital punishment was debated in Parliament, the Evans case and the events at 10 Rillington Place would be put forth as one of the main reasons to never bring it back. Fleischer's film often found itself appearing often on TV, despite its tough subject matter and bleak tone. Yes, films are primarily made for entertainment, but some are designed to get you thinking, debating and questioning. *10 Rillington Place* does that in spades.

FRANKENSTEIN AND THE MONSTER FROM HELL
Fisher's Neglected Classic

by James Lecky

In the late '50s, Hammer changed on-screen horror forever. The expressionist mood of such films as *Dr. Jekyll and Mr. Hyde* (1931), *Dracula* (1931) and James Whale's *Frankenstein* (1931) was replaced by bright Eastmancolor and a willingness to bring more graphic bloodletting and violence to the screen (at least in contemporary terms).

Prior to the release of *The Curse of Frankenstein* (1957), Hammer had merely been one of a number of British film studios producing cheap and cheerful entertainment for the masses. Comedy, crime, drama and melodrama, science fiction, war movies, Hammer's remit was a wide one - and always with a careful eye kept upon the budget. The success of *The Quatermass Xperiment* (1955), based on Nigel Kneale's ground-breaking BBC serial, convinced the higher-ups at Hammer that there was money to be made in horror.

The Curse of Frankenstein, starring Peter Cushing as the eponymous Baron and Christopher Lee as his Creation, ushered in a new era for Hammer. Increasingly thereafter, the studio would be closely associated with the horror genre. *Dracula* (aka *The Horror of Dracula*) (1958) - also starring Cushing and Lee - cemented the association and, for roughly the next two decades, Hammer's output would encompass vampires, monster-makers, zombies, gorgons and satanists, instigating a revival of gothic horror in both Europe (e.g. *Black Sunday*, 1960)

His brain came from a genius. His body came from a killer. His soul came from hell!

Your blood will run cold when the monster rises.

Paramount Pictures presents
A Hammer Production
FRANKENSTEIN AND THE MONSTER FROM HELL
starring
Peter Cushing Shane Briant Screenplay by John Elder Produced by Roy Skeggs
Directed by Terence Fisher Prints by Movielab In Color A Paramount Picture

and the United States, particularly Roger Corman's Poe Cycle beginning with *House of Usher* (1960) and ending with *The Tomb of Ligeia* (1964).

By the early '70s, however, Hammer was in trouble. Rising production costs impacted on the notoriously frugal studio's output. Its principle stars were either aging (in the case of Peter Cushing) or growing increasingly dissatisfied with the roles on offer (Christopher Lee had come to loathe Dracula, seeing the character as a millstone rather than a milestone). Worse than that, the studio's output had begun to look rather old-fashioned in the face of new and more radical horrors, in particular two films, both released in 1968, that provided the same cultural shock which Hammer had unleashed a decade earlier.

Roman Polanski's *Rosemary's Baby* and George A. Romero's *Night of the Living Dead* brought horror firmly into the modern age. Polanski's tale of devil-worship and the anti-Christ is set not in the fairytale Mittel Europa so beloved of Hammer, but in urban New York, while Romero's film - inspired at least in part by *The Plague of the Zombies* (1966) - brought a new and explicit eye for violence to the screen. Moreover, both films rejected the notion of Good overcoming Evil, with the forces of chaos seemingly triumphant by the final frames.

Against this, Hammer had tried, sometimes rather

successfully, to diversify their basic formula with the likes of *Hands of the Ripper* (1971), *Dr. Jekyll and Sister Hyde* (1971), *Dracula AD 1972* (1972), *Demons of the Mind* (1972), *Vampire Circus* (1972), *The Legend of the Seven Golden Vampires* (1974) and Brian Clemens' remarkable *Captain Kronos, Vampire Hunter* (1974). While some of these films hold a place in the hearts of Hammer aficionados, critical and audience reaction to them at the time was, at best, mixed.

Moreover, an attempt to refresh the ongoing Frankenstein series - *The Horror of Frankenstein* (1970) starring Ralph Bates (groomed to be Hammer's new leading man) - had proven less than successful, leading Hammer to recall their original Baron Peter Cushing, and, just as importantly the man who had helmed *The Curse of Frankenstein*, director Terence Fisher.

Eschewing the boobs 'n' bums approach of many Hammer movies of the early '70s (particularly *The Vampire Lovers*, *Twins of Evil* and *Lust for a Vampire*), going instead for a much more claustrophobic feeling combined with a gleeful approach to the gore, *Frankenstein and the Monster from Hell* (daft title to one side) manages to be a final, joyfully bloody roll of the dice for the traditional Hammer movie.

Following in the footsteps of his idol Victor Frankenstein, Dr. Simon Helder (Shane Briant) is arrested for sorcery and sentenced to imprisonment in an insane asylum. Here he meets the mysterious Dr. Victor (Peter Cushing) who is soon revealed to be Frankenstein, alive and well and practically in charge of the institution.

Helder finds himself taken under the wing of the now clearly insane Frankenstein, his hands ruined in a fire (presumably the same fire that ended *Frankenstein Must Be Destroyed*, 1969) and together they continue the Baron's experiments to cheat death and create life. Fortunately, the asylum is a rich source of raw materials - a hulking ape-like, homicidal inmate here, an insane sculptor there and, most importantly, the brain of an only slightly deranged violin-playing genius to top it all off. In time honoured fashion, nothing quite goes to plan and instead of creating a violin-playing genius they create a revenge-fuelled madman Schneider (played by Darth-Vader-to-be David Prowse, who had previously played the Creature in *The Horror of Frankenstein*) who is eventually torn to pieces by the other inmates after a murderous and hugely entertaining killing spree.

Cushing is excellent as usual, his Frankenstein now a man prepared to go to any lengths and his insanity bubbling under the surface for all to see. Briant (as icy and imperious here as in *Captain Kronos, Vampire Hunter*) exudes the same chilling charm the younger Cushing demonstrated in *The Curse of Frankenstein*, John Stratton as the oily Asylum Director is enough to give anyone a delicious shudder of disgust, and Madeline Smith as the mute Sarah/Angel, Frankenstein's erstwhile assistant, brings vulnerability to

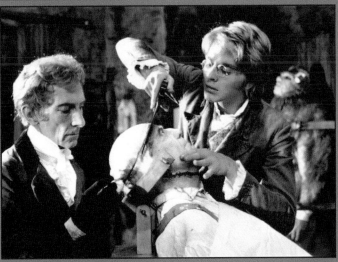

what might have been simply a decorative role.

But it is the inmates of the asylum themselves who create the essentially uneasy atmosphere of the film - the strangely camp Transvest (Michael Ward), dressed in lavender who flits in and out of several scenes, Mueller (Sydney Bromley) an old man "who believes himself to be God", first seen mock-crucified against his cell wall, Tarmut (Bernard Lee - the original M in the Bond films - in a wordless, poignant cameo), a sculptor who's brain has "atrophied rapidly", and the cackling women and howling men who could have come straight from Peter Weiss' *Marat/Sade*.

Added to this is Fisher's unflinching eye - always a feature of his best films, here given free reign by the relaxation of British censorship laws. The hanging of Professor Durendel (Charles Lloyd-Pack) with his own violin strings, a skull sawn open, jars of staring eyeballs, the Baron's perfunctory treatment of a discarded brain and the brutal death of the creature all bring an unsettling feeling to the film, best summed up in the moment when the frustrated Baron, cursing his crippled hands, holds a severed artery in his teeth to assist Helder in an operation to attach Durendel's hand to the hulking Schneider's wrist: "You see, it *can* be done." A powerful scene which is often truncated.

The film is not without its flaws, however, and there are times when the low-budget is all-too apparent - the miniature shots of the asylum are unconvincing, the make-up for the creature is less than satisfactory (though Prowse still manages to convey a certain pathos at times), the sets have an aspect of cardboard and polystyrene, and the rich

Eastmancolor that had been such a feature of the earlier movies is here replaced with a dull if fitting autumnal grey, brown and green colour palette - but what elevates it are the performances from both the stars and supporting cast. Cushing is as athletic as ever and there are moments which knowingly recall his previous outings as both the Baron and Professor Van Helsing ("Ah, Kidneys? Oh! Delicious" might be seen as a counterpart to the "Pass the marmalade" quip in *The Curse of Frankenstein*). The moment he leaps upon the rampaging Creature's back to subdue it with ether has parallels with the famous climax of *Dracula*.

This is not to say that either Cushing, Fisher or screenwriter John Elder (aka Hammer stalwart and Jack-of-most-trades, Anthony Hinds) are content to rehash past glories, but rather that they knew what made the best Hammer films work so well - a little gore, a little humour, some familiar faces (former Dr. Who Patrick Troughton appears as a body snatcher, and perennial screen-policeman Norman Mitchell turns up as... well, a policeman).

Briant, like Ralph Bates, was seen by some as the heir-apparent to Cushing's Hammer crown. As well as the previously mentioned *Captain Kronos*, he had appeared in the odd psychodrama *Straight on Till Morning* (1972) alongside Rita Tushingham, then in a typically aristocratic role in *Demons of the Mind,* and shortly after as the title

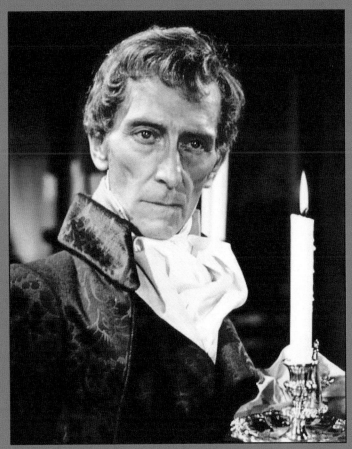

character of the Dan Curtis production *The Picture of Dorian Gray* (1973) for U.S television. *Frankenstein and the Monster from Hell* is one of his finest screen performances and his predicament here - torn between his devotion to science and his own moral sensibilities - illustrates the notion of "hubris clobbered by nemesis" (as coined by British author Brian Aldiss) so central to the Frankenstein story.

Madeline Smith was, in many ways, the archetypal '70s dolly bird, often cast in comedies as the Object of Desire for lecherous older men or as ditsy young things, but her eloquently mute performance as Angel shows that her abilities were often underused and underappreciated. Her other horror credits include *Taste the Blood of Dracula* (1970), *The Vampire Lovers* (1970), *Tam Lin* (1970), the Vincent Price camp classic *Theatre of Blood* (1973), and she was Miss Caruso in the massively entertaining Bond meets blaxploitation film *Live and Let Die* (1973).

Peter Cushing needs, or should need, little introduction to fans of classic British horror. He was, simply, a consummate screen actor. He brought considerable skill, gravitas and professionalism to his work for Hammer, Amicus and many others. As an actor he will always be closely associated with horror films (although his scene-stealing turn as the imperious Grand Moff Tarkin in *Star Wars* [1977] has probably assured his lasting fame). Victor Frankenstein was his finest screen role and he played the Baron six times for Hammer.

Fisher was one of the greatest directors of British

horror, a man whose work was initially dismissed by critics but whose critical reputation is, at long last, being re-evaluated. Something of a journeyman director until he found his niche, his work for Hammer (the Baron and the Count not withstanding), includes a number of bona fide classics - not least *The Curse of the Werewolf* (1961), *The Devil Rides Out* (1968) and *The Hound of the Baskervilles* (1959) which gave Cushing one of his best roles as Sherlock Holmes - but some of his minor work, such as *Island of Terror* (1966) or *Night of the Big Heat* (1967), both produced for the short-lived Planet Films, are gems. Even such misfires as *The Man Who Could Cheat Death* (1959) and *The Two Faces of Dr Jekyll* (1960) are visually arresting films.

Completed in 1972 but unreleased until 1974, where it played second fiddle on double bills with *Captain Kronos*, *Frankenstein and the Monster from Hell* is, in many ways, a film of lasts. It was Fisher's final film (he would pass away in 1980 at the age of 76), the final time that Cushing would play the Baron for Hammer, and the last time that Hammer would revisit their Mittel Europa cinematic landscape unadorned by other considerations. It also marked the penultimate Hammer score from James Bernard who had provided memorable music for so many of their films.

Dismissed or simply ignored by critics at the time, *Frankenstein and the Monster from Hell* is a muted yet beautifully fitting swansong for the film cycle.

As the Baron says, surveying the remains of his broken and bloodied creation:

"It's all over now. All over. . . But, next time. . ."

Rachel Bellwoar examines Rainer Werner Fassbinder's
DESPAIR

It's always interesting to see which details a director or screenwriter latches onto when adapting a book for the big screen. In Vladimir Nabokov's novel 'Despair', goggle-moggles only appear once and it's not a particularly memorable scene. Yet, for the opening credits of director Rainer Werner Fassbinder and screenwriter Tom Stoppard's film adaptation, Hermann's wife Lydia (Andréa Ferréol) is shown making goggle-moggles with an emphasis on the eggshells being dropped into the sink. Since the sink has a leaky faucet (or at least that's the suggestion - technically Fassbinder's camera is so close-up on the shells it's only an assumption that they're in the sink and not on the counter, being dripped on by some leak in the ceiling), one of the eggshells keeps perpetually shaking.

For those unfamiliar with goggle-moggles (a dessert), they don't get named until later when Lydia's cousin Ardalion (Volker Spengler) protests that Hermann (Dirk Bogarde) is getting his "goggle-moggle", when Lydia made one for each of them, but its inclusion isn't without significance. Hermann is a Russian émigré to Berlin, and goggle-moggle (as it's spelled in the book) is the Russian name for the dessert. In Jewish communities in Central Europe where the dessert originated, it's referred to as kogel mogel.

Whereas Nabokov's novel (which was serialized in 1934, before being published in 1936) doesn't dwell as much on the rise of fascism that was going on in Germany at the time, this is definitely a preoccupation of Fassbinder and Stoppard's movie. At work, Hermann makes cracks when his colleague, Müller (Peter Kern), shows up in a Nazi uniform ("Have you joined the boy scouts are something?") and later, while making the critical decision to reach out to his alleged doppelganger Felix (Klaus Löwitsch), Hermann witnesses a Jewish business being vandalized across the street. In any other world, Hermann putting his plan to murder Felix into motion and pass Felix off as himself so he can cash in on his life insurance policy would be the craziest thing going on in this scene, but by contrasting his actions with the flagrant anti-Semitism going on by the Nazis, it's all relative. The world has gone mad, and when Fassbinder turns the camera back on Hermann, it's no wonder the angle is askew.

Despair would be Fassbinder's first English-language film and stars British icon Dirk Bogarde. According to Bogarde's biographer John Coldstream in his book 'Dirk Bogarde: The Authorized Biography': "...the script [originally] called for Hermann... both to drive and to appear in the nude. ... The driving was easily dealt with;

the nudity became briefly something of an issue." Knowing this, it does explain why Bogarde remains conspicuously clothed in this movie. One of the very first scenes is of Hermann preparing to make love to his wife. From the start, Peer Raben's music ensures that the tone is eerie and sinister, not sexy. Every time Hermann moves to undress, he comes back with more clothes on. First, it's a new robe he pulls out from under the bed. That's not so incredible. What takes this sequence into the realm of absurdity, though, is when Hermann takes off his robe but, instead of taking his T-shirt off, he returns in a fully buttoned-up pajama top (the T-shirt visible underneath).

That Hermann isn't too concerned about having sex is obvious, but he is interested in something - what Hermann in the book calls "dissociation." Basically, Hermann is able to watch himself having sex, like there are two of him in the room - one having sex and one observing. Since Nabokov's novel is written in the first person, Hermann is able to explain how this works more in the book, like how apparently the further away he is from his double, the more erotic the experience. Hermann even says: "… I never got farther back than the console in the parlor…" and that's exactly where Fassbinder positions the second Hermann in the film (both of whom are played by Bogarde, wearing different clothes).

The film is definitely vaguer than the book when it comes to clarifying whether this second Hermann is supposed to be real or a figment of the first Hermann's imagination. Even Hermann suffers a brief identity crisis as a result.

The art direction and set decoration by Jochen Schumacher, Herbert Strabel and Kathrin Brunner serves the story well, especially the decision to give Herman's

apartment glass walls. Not only are they reflective (feeding into Hermann's obsession with doppelgangers) but they're transparent. At one point Lydia makes a fuss about wanting to close the door before they have sex. Hermann tells her to keep the door open, but the pointlessness of closing a glass door for privacy is never addressed.

By creating a glass world around Hermann, *Despair* provides an explanation for why his ego is so inflated. If nothing gets past Hermann, it's because the walls around him are literally transparent, yet he doesn't see it that way. Even at work (Hermann owns a chocolate factory), the walls are made of glass so he can watch his workers go about their jobs, yet instead of recognizing that most of the world isn't designed that way, Hermann insists on his "superior" intellect. It's the kind of delusional thinking that allows someone to think they can perpetrate the perfect murder. The glass reveals his entire psychology, yet Bogarde's Hermann and Nabokov's Hermann aren't the same beast.

Bogarde may have only insisted on not driving because he didn't know how, but it does change how the character reads on screen. In the film, he is a lot more dependent on others. Instead of driving himself to work (as he does in the book), he expects Lydia to take him. Once there, Müller opens the door for him. Given that Hermann is so reliant on others, though, his sense of superiority over them comes across as more curious.

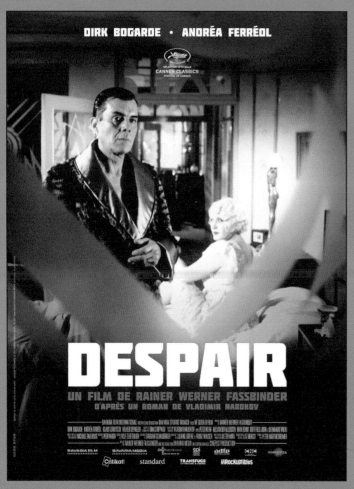

Bogarde's Hermann is also crueler than the book's, but there are reasons for that, the main of which is that, in Nabokov's novel, he is the narrator. That means he can paint whatever picture of himself that he wants, however inaccurate, and where his memories are concerned, Hermann is even upfront about mixing up some of the details. He's the definition of an unreliable narrator and, what's more, there's a big difference between thinking cruel thoughts and saying them aloud. In the film, Stoppard uses a lot of the belittling comments that Hermann only thinks in the book and has Bogarde say them aloud to the characters' faces. On the bright side, whereas Hermann in the book is oblivious to anyone ever getting the best of him, in the film you get to see that other people aren't as fooled by him as he thinks.

It all builds up to Hermann meeting his doppelganger, or the guy he is convinced looks exactly like him, but does he? In the book, Nabokov doesn't have to commit to an answer, or at least is able to hold off until the end to expose the truth. In the film, however, Fassbinder has to make a choice by casting someone else to play Felix. Of all the changes, this is the biggest, and it mostly comes down to whether you prefer your stories ambiguous or clearcut. Basically, *Despair* is *The Prince and the Pauper* if the Prince intended to murder the Pauper for life insurance money. Throw in a failed Harpo Marx mirror routine from *Duck Soup*, and you've got yourself a show!

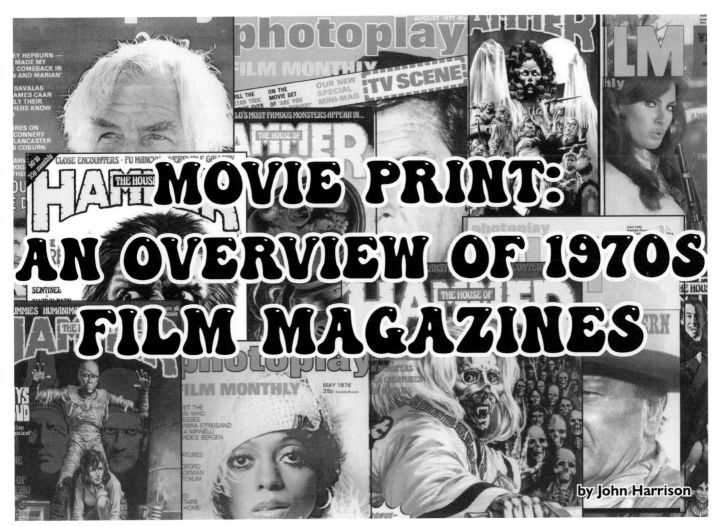

MOVIE PRINT: AN OVERVIEW OF 1970S FILM MAGAZINES

by John Harrison

Long before the internet made information and the latest news available at our fingertips, film fans had to rely in large part on the printed page to keep them up to date and fed with knowledge. For myself, it was a big part of the ritual when it came to going to the cinema as a kid in the late '70s. Every weekend trip to the movies would be preceded by a visit to Space Age Books, the cramped shop in the heart of Melbourne's inner city, which was a mecca for science-fiction, horror and fantasy fans. Armed with my hard-earned lawnmowing money, I would meet a few likeminded friends on a Saturday morning and we would invade Space Age, each of us heading for our favourite sections. I went straight to the magazine rack at the rear of the shop, which would be fully stocked with an eye-popping assortment of genre film publications, both the glossy professional titles as well as the lower-budgeted fanzines. I'd scoop up the latest issues of 'Starlog', 'Famous Monsters of Filmland' and whatever else took my fancy, then we would all head to the cinema, buy our tickets and sit silently in the lobby as we poured over our newly acquired goodies while waiting for the movie to begin.

While movie magazines have existed for almost as long as movies themselves, the '70s seemed to be a particularly rich and fertile period for them, with the range of titles and variety of genres they covered incredibly diverse.

If you were a fan of genre cinema, it was a particularly memorable golden age. Of the more mainstream magazines, the British edition of 'Photoplay' was certainly one of the best of the '70s. First published In 1951, it was an offshoot of the American magazine of the same name, which had been around since 1911. Aesthetically, the UK edition of 'Photoplay' had vibrant covers and beautiful, very '70s fonts and layouts, and the text was quite small, meaning they could cram more in-depth pieces into each issue (though it's a tactic which makes it a bit tough on the eyes these days).

Over in the US, 'American Cinematographer' was one of the better and more respected film publications. Focusing heavily on the photographic side of things, 'American Cinematographer' presented in-depth articles, along with many behind-the-scenes photos not seen elsewhere, covering not only the big blockbuster movies of the decade but also smaller productions and documentaries. It had special issues devoted to the Oscars and subjects like new special effects and photographic techniques, a look at the burgeoning Zoetrope Studios, films from a certain exotic corner of the globe, and more. People who know me would not be surprised to discover that amongst my favourite issues of 'American Cinematographer' is the June 1977 edition, which features an excellent cover article of

the filming of *Rollercoaster* (1977).

Australia had its own film magazine named 'Cinema Papers', a larger tabloid-sized title that was first published in January of 1974, with one of its three founders being filmmaker Philippe Mora. Arriving just in time for both the new wave of Australian cinema, as well as the more low-brow Ozploitation films, 'Cinema Papers' had a strong local flavour but still had a lot of international content. One of the most sought-after issues of 'Cinema Papers' from that period would have to be no. 21 from May-June 1979, which featured one of the first in-depth cover features on a new local movie called *Mad Max*.

Let's take a closer look at some of the more specialized film magazines which the '70s had to offer.

Genre Publications

Horror movie fans faced no shortage of reading material during the '70s, being particularly spoiled for choice during the first half of the decade. The monster craze that swept through the '60s had certainly levelled off, but there was still enough interest to make some publishers persevere, and horror was a perennially popular genre amongst moviegoers. 'Famous Monsters of Filmland', the publication which was most influential in spearheading the monster revival with its first issue

back in 1958, was still around to introduce '70s kids to the world of horror cinema. Published by James Warren and driven by the bad puns of editor Forrest J. Ackerman, 'Famous Monsters' by this point was comprised of a lot of reprints from earlier issues, and while the magazine still relied heavily on films and stars of the past, it still covered its share of the latest fright flicks with movies like *Frogs* (1972), *Westworld* (1973), *Madhouse* (1974), *Food of the Gods* (1976) and many others getting cover features. And there were still plenty of 'Famous Monsters' clones popping up, like Marvel's 'Monsters of the Movies', 'Quasimodo's Monster

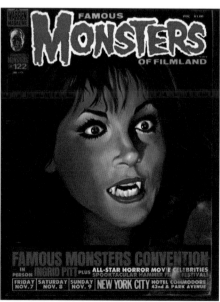

Magazine', 'Movie Monsters' and the newspaper-like 'The Monster Times'.

For those older readers who wanted something a bit more in-depth and varied, there was 'Castle of Frankenstein', published infrequently between 1962 and 1975 and edited by the enigmatic Calvin Beck (supposedly one of the main inspirations for Robert Bloch's Norman Bates character). American genre fanzines were also entering a real golden age in the early '70s, thanks to titles like 'Photon', 'Gore Creatures' (later 'Midnight Marquee'), the Hammer-centric 'Little Shoppe of Horrors' (still going strong in 2023) and Fred Clarke's 'Cinefantastique', a much more opinionated publication

that went more pro as the decade wore on. July 1979 also saw the first issue of 'Fangoria', though that title would exert more impact and influence the following decade.

The UK had its own answers to 'Famous Monsters' in 'World of Horror' and 'The House of Hammer'. Debuting in 1974 and published on semi-gloss paper with a substantial amount of colour, and in a slightly taller format than most standard monster magazines, 'World of Horror' was certainly an eye-catching publication, featuring a nice mixture of 'Famous Monsters'-style nostalgia alongside the more gruesome modern horror that was becoming prevalent by the early '70s, as well as some original

short fiction and art. Being a UK magazine, Hammer horror naturally has a strong presence within the pages of 'World of Horror', and despite its title it also delved into sci-fi territory on occasion, with cover features devoted to *Star Trek* as well as several articles on *Dr. Who* and the various creatures who appeared in the long-running series. The magazine at times ventured even further from horror territory with articles on films like Irwin Allen's disaster classic *The Towering Inferno* (1974).

For their covers, 'World of Horror' eschewed the use of any original art and relied instead on bold, full-page

photographs usually featuring a close-up of a character's face - be it Christopher Lee's lightning-charred features from the climax of *Scars of Dracula* (1970), Leonard Nimoy's Spock or John Huston's stately simian Lawgiver from *Battle for the Planet of the Apes* (1973).

While 'World of Horror' only lasted for nine issues, 'The House of Hammer' enjoyed more longevity, with twenty-three issues published between 1976 and 1978. Founded and published by Dez Skinn, the magazine's title gave away the primary focus of its contents. Featuring some absolutely stunning painted covers (most by Brian Lewis), the black-and-white interiors of 'The House of Hammer' featured a balance of articles, interviews and news, with each issue highlighted by a comic book adaptation of a Hammer classic (usually, the film featured on that issue's cover). The comic adaptations were quite exceptional and moody, with beautiful art contributed by such names as Brian Bolland, John Bolton, Brian Lewis, Paul Neary and others. The cool thing about 'The House of Hammer' was that the comic adaptations allowed younger fans to experience the movie in a way (remember, in the early '70s there was no home video, television prints were usually butchered when they screened, and most Hammer horror flicks were still given an X rating in the UK). Some of the Hammer movies that were given the comic book treatment in 'The House of Hammer' were *The Gorgon* (1964), *Moon Zero Two* (1969), *Twins of Evil* (1971),

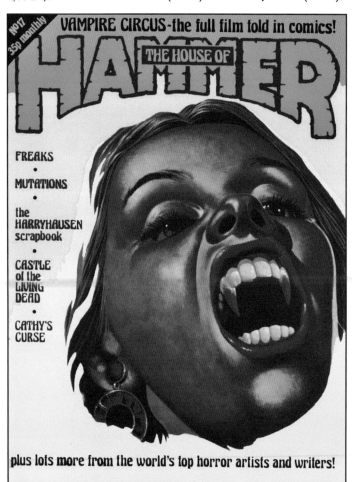

Vampire Circus (1972) and many more, including several of their Dracula, Frankenstein and Quatermass movies. In the US, 'The House of Hammer' was published under the less-specific title of 'House of Horror' before it suddenly ceased publication in 1978. Skinn briefly resurrected the magazine as 'Halls of Horror' in 1982 with Dave Reeder as editor.

Once *Star Wars* (1977) hit, many of the monster magazines folded, and in their place came a slew of new titles devoted to the space adventure craze which the movie singlehandedly kickstarted. 'Starlog', which first appeared in August of 1976 and was primarily focused on *Star Trek* for its early issues, became the flagship for American science-fiction cinema magazines and, post *Star Wars*, it was quickly followed by other publications like 'Fantastic Films', 'Science Fantasy Film Classics' and a virtual avalanche of cheap titles published by the notorious Myron Fass. Fass was a New York publisher who dabbled in everything from horror comics to true crime to rock and roll. He was always quick to jump on a trend, and in the late '70s busied himself grinding out low-rent magazines with generic, cash-in titles like 'Space Wars', 'Space Trek', 'Star Warp' and 'Star Encounters'.

Over in the UK, even 'The House of Hammer' broke with tradition and put *Star Wars* on the cover of their sixteenth issue, leading Dez Skinn to launch a new magazine 'Starburst' in December 1977. With 'Starlog' as its clear template, the success of 'Starburst' was so impressive that

Marvel recruited Skinn to head up the UK branch of their comics division.

Souvenir Programs

The souvenir program was a popular piece of movie memorabilia for several decades, being particularly prevalent during the '50s, '60s and '70s, when just about any film that got a cinema release had its own souvenir program published. Similar in concept to concert and theatre programs, the movie programs usually comprised of around twenty pages, and while most were of a large 9x12 inches, they did come in varying dimensions. Printed on thick glossy stock, the interior would comprise of an assortment of stills from the movie, a basic plot synopsis, profiles of the main stars as well as the director/writer/producer, with a more complete credit list on the inside back cover.

For the most part, souvenir programs were sold exclusively at the cinema screening the film in question though sometimes they would turn up on newsstands or advertised for sale in magazines like 'Starlog' (possibly returned stock looking to be moved on). A lot of programs also included an address to send a couple of dollars to if you wanted an additional copy (many of them seem to be published in New York by various companies).

Of particular appeal, especially to collectors, are the Japanese programs, which often boasted rare photos and some wild covers and interior designs. While the souvenir programs would continue on into the early '80s, they became a lot less common as the decade wore on before disappearing altogether.

In-House Magazines

In Australia during the '70s, the two big cinema chains, Hoyts and Village, both published their own quarterly in-house magazines in order to promote their latest, and upcoming, releases. Hoyts had 'Movie News', while Village had 'Movie 71-79' (the relevant year of publication was added to each issue's title). 'Movie News' and 'Movie' were sold both at the cinema box-office and snack bar as well as on local newsstands. Naturally, as each magazine was promoting a particular distributor's product, there was very little crossover between the two titles.

The in-house magazines weren't unique to Australia, with similar publications popping up in a number of countries. Singapore, for example, had its own magazine called 'Movie News', which was published by the Shaw Brothers, Hong Kong's biggest production and distribution facility at the time. Much like the Japanese souvenir programs, issues of this version of 'Movie News' make nice collectibles because of their exotic nature and the eclectic selection of films which made their covers, which included *The House that Dripped Blood (1972)*, *Piranha* (1978) and *Star Crash* (1978, known here under the highly original title of *Star Battle Encounters*).

One-Shot Publications

The one-shot magazines were effectively similar to the souvenir programs, except they usually had a lot more pages and were sold through the traditional newsstand and bookstore distribution channels. But they were often published with the co-operation of the film studio in question, and served the same

AUSTRALIA'S OWN FILM MAGAZINE
40¢

movie news

Vol. 11, No. 3

THE TOWERING INFERNO

Registered at G.P.D., Melbourne. for transmission by post as a newspaper — Category 'B'

purpose: to get people excited about a specific new movie. Of course, while just about every mainstream film in the '70s received a souvenir program, it was mostly only the big, exciting new blockbusters that got chosen to be the subject of a one-shot magazine.

James Warren also started specialising in one-shot movie magazines in the late '70s, publishing specials on *Star Wars* (1977), *Close Encounters of the Third Kind* (1977), *Lord of the Rings* (1978), *Moonraker* (1979), *Alien* (1979) and *Meteor* (1979). Published under the "Warren Presents" banner, these one-shots often comprised of reprints from recent issues of 'Famous Monsters', along with one or two new pieces, and the usual pages of advertising for Warren products. Two other nice one-shots which Warren published in 1979 were 'Dracula '79' and 'Movie Aliens Illustrated', which covered the respective subjects in general but were clearly put out to capitalize on the *Alien* and *Dracula* films from that year.

Poster Magazines

An interesting offshoot of regular magazines, poster magazines enjoyed a run of popularity in the '70s. The idea behind the format was simple: the package looks like a regular magazine when on the stands, in terms of its page size and cover designs, but, instead of it containing stapled pages, the whole thing was printed on one single large sheet of glossy colour paper, with one side generally containing a single image as a poster, while the reverse page had several short articles on whatever subject that particular poster magazine was dedicated to, usually accompanied by smaller photos. The whole thing was then folded several times and marketed as both a magazine and a poster, giving young teenagers (the typical target audience) more bang for their pocket money. The dimensions of the poster when unfolded was about the same as a standard one-sheet movie poster, although some were slightly larger.

The earliest and best of the genre poster magazines was the simply titled 'Monster Mag', which was published by Top Sellers in the UK, though issues were also printed in several languages for European distribution. Running for seventeen issues between 1973 and 1976, the content of 'Monster Mag' was very English and specifically very Hammer-heavy, one of the reasons why it such a desirable title for collectors of the famous British fright factory. It also didn't shy away from utilizing some of the more visceral movie stills available, leading it to carry an 'Adults Only' warning on the cover (something which of course would have only served to give it a sense of forbidden fruit, increasing its desirability amongst the underage horror-loving youngsters).

While the first issue of 'Monster Mag' no doubt raised the ire of some concerned parents, it was the follow-up which really ran into trouble. When the English language copies of 'Monster Mag' #2 arrived in the UK from the printers in Italy, they were deemed to be offensive and all copies were seized and destroyed by officers from Her Majesty's Customs and Excise, leading it to become the most sought-after issue of the magazine (copies of the European version occasionally show up at high prices). Looking at it today, it's difficult to place what exactly the UK customs saw so wrong with the issue to ban and destroy it. There's nothing overly gory about it. Maybe someone was just in a bad or easily outraged mood that day, or they took offense at that issue's 'Focus on Freaks' angle, which seemed a tad more lurid and provocative than the usual cinematic vampires, werewolves and Frankenstein monsters. The poster for this issue does feature a rather ghoulish image of one of the unfortunate title characters from Jack Cardiff's effective oddity *The Mutations* (1974), and one of the interior articles carried a photo of the human-headed dog from *The Mephisto Waltz* (1971), either of which may have upset the delicate sensibilities of the deciders of good taste. To play it safe and not risk a repeat incident, a local UK printer was soon found and utilized for future issues.

While the covers, articles and interior posters for 'Monster Mag' were predominately Hammer-centric (with Christopher Lee a clear favourite), it still managed to cover a few non-Hammer oddities like *Beware! The Blob* (1972), *Blacula* (1972), Larry Cohen's *It's Alive* (1974) and William Grefe's strange swamp horror cheapie *Death Curse of Tartu* (1966). *The Exorcist* (1973) also warranted some coverage, as did some UK horror films that were not produced by Hammer but clearly inspired by them, such as Freddie Francis' underrated *The Creeping Flesh* (1973).

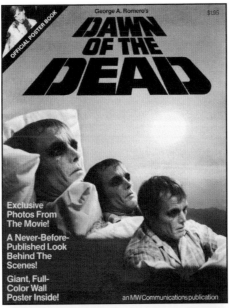

Other poster magazines appeared during the '70s devoted to movies like *The Rocky Horror Picture Show* (1975), *The Island of Dr. Moreau* (1977), *Grease* (1977), *Saturday Night Fever* (1978) and the *Planet of the Apes* series, while the much-hyped *King Kong* (1976) was deemed worthy of two different poster magazines (one covered the whole history of Kong to that point, while the other focused solely on the 1976 version). Most movie poster magazines were one-shots, with a few exceptions. Movies like *Close Encounters of the Third Kind*, *Alien* and *Star Trek: The Motion Picture* were popular enough to warrant at least two issues of their respective poster magazines, while the 'Star Wars Official Poster Monthly' ran for a whopping eighteen issues (with a further nine issues published under the '80s sequels titles).

Perhaps one of the most unexpected poster magazines from the period was the one-shot published by MW Communications to tie-in with George A. Romero's classic zombie epic *Dawn of the Dead* (1978), which featured articles and a beautiful two-page interior art spread by Jim Weholer, along with a main poster by Ron Mahoney. Certainly, a great piece of original merchandise from this landmark and highly influential film. Another title sought after by

collectors is the poster magazine for Walter Hill's urban gang classic *The Warriors* (1979), which was published by Paradise Press.

While most poster magazines were devoted to fantasy, sci-fi and horror cinema, other films did receive the poster magazine treatment, especially if the film in question was a hit with the teen audience. *Saturday Night Fever* and *Grease* received poster magazines. There was also 'Kung-Fu Monthly', a British poster magazine which ran from 1973 to 1979, a rather phenomenal run. Though ostensibly devoted to martial arts in general, it was for all intents and purposes a Bruce Lee magazine, with the then recently deceased star

featured prominently on the cover - if not on the poster - of just about every issue. 'Kung-Fu Monthly' did occasionally feature other martial arts film stars, such as Angela Mao, the Taiwanese actress who appeared in *Deadly China Doll* (1972), *Hapkido* (1972), *Lady Whirlwind* (1972), *Enter the Dragon* (1972) and many others, who shared the cover of issue number four with Lee (at least on the UK edition, the American printing had Lee only on the cover). Offsetting the film-related text were instructional articles and diagrams aimed at budding martial artists. It's easy to see why 'Kung-Fu Monthly'

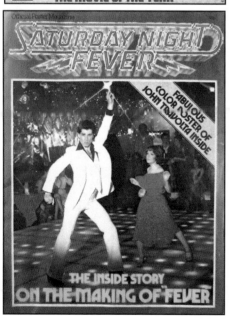

continued to focus primarily on Lee, since it became the world's best-selling martial arts magazine for a while, and spawned several imitators, the best of which was likely 'Dragon', another UK poster magazine which featured several crossover film stars such as Jim Kelly and David Carradine on its covers and posters.

Comic Adaptations

While comic book adaptations of films, published in the standard comic book size and format, had been around since the '50s, Marvel would start to issue quite a few movie adaptations in the larger magazine size during the mid '70s. Apart from their continuing 'Planet of the Apes' comic magazine, they also published one-shot adaptations of *Close Encounters of the Third Kind*, *Jaws 2*, *Meteor* and *Star Trek: The Motion Picture*, as part of their 'Marvel Comics Super Special' line. The comic adaptations provided another way for fans to relive the magic of the movie, and most of them contained photos and articles/ interviews related to the film in question, giving them an additional appeal and visual flair.

Naturally, this article only scratches the surface of the subject's vast range, but it will hopefully provide a useful overview and starting off point for those wishing to dive deeper, or bring a nostalgic smile to those who were there to read these magazines at the time and are now having that same passion and feeling revived and fulfilled within the pages of 'Cinema of the '70s'.

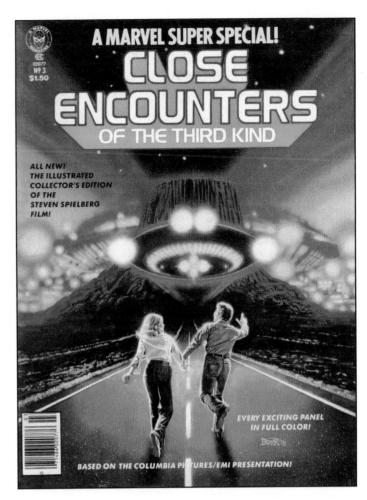

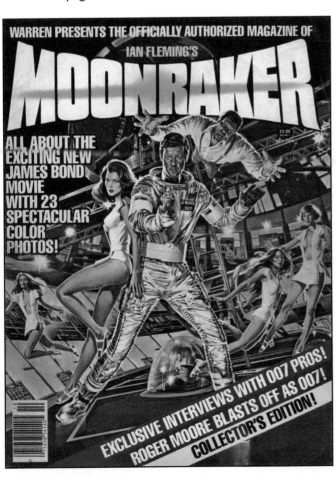

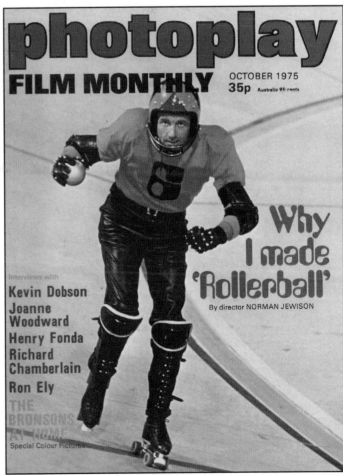

CAPRICORN ONE
A Funny Thing Happened on the Way to Mars...

by James Cadman

If someone asks you for a brief synopsis of *Capricorn One*, just for kicks tell them it's about a mission to Mars and nothing more. And then tell them to watch the film. If you haven't seen it yourself, do so before reading this article as it's packed with spoilers.

The movie opens with a shot of a spacecraft on the launch pad at Cape Canaveral. Spectators, including the astronauts' families, politicians and television crews, watch from miles away as *Capricorn One*, the first manned flight to Mars, prepares for lift-off.

Onboard are three astronauts; Col. Charles Brubaker (James Brolin), Lt. Col. Peter Willis (Sam Waterston) and Commander John Walker (O.J. Simpson). Everything appears normal until, in the middle of the countdown, they are suddenly ushered from the capsule and flown to a top-secret government facility deep in a southwestern desert. The programme director, Dr Kelloway (Hal Holbrook), explains to the crew that, just weeks before the launch, a contractor had supplied a faulty life-support system. Had they remained aboard, they wouldn't have survived more than three days. Kelloway tells the men it is too late to cancel the mission without undermining the whole space programme. With NASA funding under threat, Congress is determined to restore the public's interest in the programme. So the launch goes ahead and, unbeknownst to television audiences around the world, an empty rocket is propelled to the Red Planet.

The astronauts soon learn that a bomb has been planted on the plane carrying their families from Florida back to Texas. Left with no choice but to comply, they find themselves at the heart of an elaborate deception to simulate the landing on a soundstage deep in the desert.

All appears to be going to plan until we hear that a defective heatshield on the unmanned craft has caused it to burn up on re-entry and the men soon realise they are expendable. Still in their NASA overalls, they make a daring escape and spend the second half of the film on the run, hotly pursued by enemy agents in menacing military helicopters.

With post-Watergate notions of collusion and cover-up, *Capricorn One* flirts with the popular conspiracy theory that the moon landing of July 1969 was a monumental fake. The film cleverly plays to a manifestly '70s distrust in US government departments and agencies - a sentiment of apathy and cynicism towards authority that still exists today.

Although he conceived the premise for *Capricorn One* in 1972, writer-director Peter Hyams didn't secure interest in his script until 1976. By this time, the events surrounding Richard Nixon's downfall had already filtered through to the American psyche and were influencing a popular genre of political thrillers.

Back at the time of the moon landing, Hyams was working for CBS producing TV documentaries devoted to the Apollo missions. Reflecting on this experience, he clearly found the prospect of an elaborate hoax quite

delicious: "Whenever there was something on the news about a space shuttle, they would cut to a studio in St. Louis where there was a simulation of what was going on. I wondered what would happen if someone faked a whole story."

The media's role in perpetuating such theories cannot be underestimated. In his study of American popular culture 'The Dream Life', J Hoberman refers to the Apollo 11 mission as "a triumph of intellect." Taking place the same year as Woodstock, Hoberman refers to them as "uniquely participatory media events." He describes how one commentator cynically claimed that the whole moon expedition could easily have been acted out on the backlot of Universal Studios.

Hyams has since stated he has no reason to doubt the landing was real. While there is overwhelming evidence that all NASA moon landings happened and no cause to believe anything was faked for political gain, he nonetheless saw *Capricorn One* as a timely pushback on the instinctive belief that anything anybody sees on TV is automatically real. In a similar vein, when interviewed on location back in 1977, James Brolin jumped on the bandwagon with his assertion that: "We watch a lot of television and we read a lot of newspapers and we tend to accept the fact that something is on television or in the newspapers as proof that it's true. Well, it's not. I think the real danger is in not finding out for ourselves - or at least not trying to investigate further."

Hyams once said he would have loved the film to open with the line "This picture was made despite the efforts of NASA." Despite the film's cynical attitude towards NASA, the space agency cooperated fully with the production, even loaning a prototype of its Apollo command module to be used in the picture. Indeed, it is worth considering whether the unashamedly flawed use of a rickety Apollo-era command module and lunar module for a Mars mission was deliberate. Could we speculate that the implausibility of this whole set-up suggested that NASA felt that *not* cooperating with the production would somehow endorse Hyams' outlandish story? Perhaps they saw it as one giant leap too far.

Capricorn One is an immensely personal film to me. I fondly recall watching it on TV with my dad late one evening in the '90s. As a young teenager, it is one of the first films I remember seeing on the small screen and one I went to great lengths to locate on VHS. For me, this is the perfect time in your life to discover this film; you're old enough to be curious about the dark, often sinister plot, yet young enough to be amused by the witty dialogue and suspend your disbelief at the events unfolding on screen.

The one character whose exploits demand perhaps the greatest suspension of disbelief is intrepid reporter Robert Caulfield, played by Elliott Gould. He is given a tip-off from one of his friends (conveniently a mission control technician) that transmissions from the shuttle are too close to be coming from space. After asking too many questions in the control room, the friend mysteriously vanishes off the face of the earth. Beginning to suspect he has stumbled upon something huge, Caulfield starts to investigate and soon finds himself the target of faceless assassins.

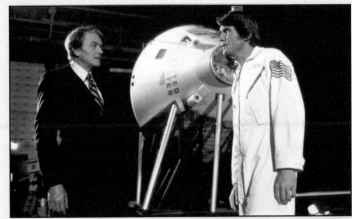

Credibility is somewhat thrown out of the window when it comes to the extent of the cover-up. For their plans to succeed, the architects behind the setup must have bought off hundreds of people. Having masterminded such a complex operation, the audience is then left wondering how they could be so inept in their attempts to sabotage Caulfield's car (an exciting sequence shot in Long Beach, California) and later to shoot him at close range.

Despite the forgivable flaws in his character's storyline, Gould is excellent and eminently watchable. His scenes with Brenda Vaccaro, as Brubaker's bereaved wife helping him uncover the truth, are beautifully written and portrayed with a warmth and sensitivity. In a hark back to his comedic persona from the likes of *California Split* and *M*A*S*H*, we delight in his witty exchanges with fellow reporter Karen Black (in a role originally chalked for Candice Bergen) and, perhaps best of all, David Doyle, as his sarcastic editor. In a scene reminiscent of a '40s film noir, Caulfield's editor springs him from jail after he is framed for drug possession before begrudgingly being told he has "24 hours to come up with something." It feels over-blown and clichéd but it's great fun and, at this stage in the plot, no one cares.

Having uncovered the 'scoop of the century', Caulfield sets off to scour the rugged desert in the hope of finding the missing astronauts. One more amusing encounter awaits him as he commissions the services of smart-mouthed crop-dusting pilot Telly Savalas, in a brief cameo. Financing the production, Lew Grade insisted on casting Savalas; he had pre-sold the film to various television networks and knew that Savalas' name, at the height of his Kojak fame, would net an extra $500,000 in TV revenue.

While pleasantly amusing, Savalas' appearance is arguably one of the weaker moments in the picture. Unfortunately, the same can be said for the three heroic astronauts. Simpson and Waterston's characters are never fully developed, making it harder to empathise with their plight. Brolin's Brubaker is better but most of his dialogue scenes are overshadowed by Holbrook who turns in a captivating performance as the villainous Kelloway. His passion and

duty are brilliantly offset against his cold, calculating wickedness as he is seen on the phone communicating with the killers he has sent to pick off the innocent crew.

In terms of its technical credits, *Capricorn One* doesn't disappoint. The cinematography is ably handled by the late Bill Butler, who had previously lensed *The Conversation*, *Jaws* and *One Flew Over the Cuckoo's Nest*. His camera and lighting serve to enhance the gritty, documentary-like atmosphere, especially during the film's opening half-hour when the scene is being set for the ultimate deception. Butler serves up two memorable zoom out shots - one of the eerie soundstage from where they execute the ultimate fraud and, more powerful still, a scene where Waterston's Willis, drained and dehydrated, is seen climbing a steep cliff, only to find the two blacked-out LOH-6 Cayuse helicopters waiting for him at the summit. Terrific!

Jerry Goldsmith's pounding score is among the film's many achievements. An orchestral masterpiece, it works brilliantly to punctuate every mood in the story, from poignant family moments with Brubaker's family to suspenseful danger and adrenaline-filled action. In one memorable segment, Brubaker finds an abandoned petrol station. He forces the door open and begins rummaging around to find a coin to telephone home and alert his family. Unable to reach anyone, he sits next to the window, desperate and alone. Behind him, we see the enemy helicopters coming into shot, their arrival signalled by Goldsmith's menacing ostinato.

Undoubtedly, the most impressive action occurs during a climactic aerial chase between the black helicopters and Savalas' creaking biplane. A remarkable sequence, it is part blue-screen and part actual aerial footage of the choppers

trying to down the crop duster's plane as Brubaker clings desperately onto the wing. The sequence was orchestrated by stunt pilot Frank Tallman. Having previously masterminded daring airborne antics for the likes of *Charley Varrick* and *The Great Waldo Pepper*, he claimed that, due to the harsh canyon terrain, it was the most dangerous project he'd ever worked on. A special mount had to be invented to hold the cameras so the helicopter's pontoons could be shown hitting the plane's wings.

According to Hyams, several preview audiences stood up and cheered during the scene. Sadly, it would prove to be Tallman's last project when, just six weeks before the film's US release, he was tragically killed when his plane crashed into the mountains above Santa Ana, California.

Despite a clumsy marketing campaign, *Capricorn One* grossed $12m at the US box office, making it the most successful independently financed movie of 1978. Producer Paul N. Lazarus III fondly refers to it as a film they made "without grown-ups". With no studio executives breathing down their necks, he said they were able to put all their energy into positive effort, describing the end result, both artistically and financially, as terrific. It is superb entertainment that certainly deserves more attention than it has received over the years.

As a thought experiment *Capricorn One* feels like an exhilarating product of its time. At a time when there is much talk of remakes, I'd argue it is a film which very much belongs in the '70s and should remain so. Today, it is fascinating to revisit the movie in the advent of new technologies, not least the polarising effect of social media coverage, as well as the emergence of fake news and misinformation over the last seven years. The basic premise, that those in power will go to any lengths to avoid exposing the truth, seems even more credible today than it was 45 years ago.

SIR LEW GRADE Presents For ASSOCIATED GENERAL FILMS
ELLIOTT GOULD • JAMES BROLIN
BRENDA VACCARO • SAM WATERSTON • O.J. SIMPSON • HAL HOLBROOK
A LAZARUS/HYAMS PRODUCTION of A PETER HYAMS FILM "CAPRICORN ONE"
Panavision® KAREN BLACK as "Judy Drinkwater" and TELLY SAVALAS as "Albain"
Music by JERRY GOLDSMITH • Produced by PAUL N. LAZARUS III • Written and Directed by PETER HYAMS

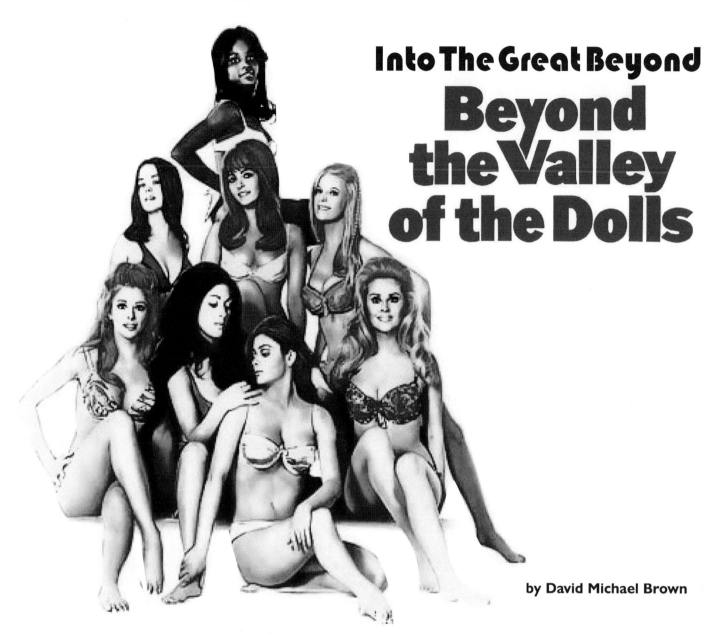

Into The Great Beyond
Beyond the Valley of the Dolls

by David Michael Brown

You can spot a Russ Meyer movie a mile away. Rapid-fire editing, snappy dialogue, righteous narration, candy-coloured cinematography, inexplicable Nazis and large-breasted women all feature heavily in the cinema of this fiercely independent filmmaker. Watching his films is like being given an instant history lesson in sexploitation cinema. Hugely influential, his particular brand of 'Bosomania' changed with the mores of the times, becoming more explicit as censorship and public tastes evolved. Many claim that despite the leering lens that focused on nudity, Meyer was a proto-feminist filmmaker, his female leads dominating his films at the expense of weak men.

I had read about Meyer's movies long before I'd seen one. 'Psychotronic Video' and 'Shock Cinema' magazines, fanzines like 'Trash City', and books like RE/Search's 'Incredibly Strange Films' all waxed lyrical about the sexploitation auteur. Luckily, thanks to the Psychotronic Video shop in Camden (no relation to the magazine) and their legendary back room, and the Scala Cinema in King's

Cross, London, who ran eye-popping Russ Meyer triple bills, my Meyer education was enabled if not complete and I started looking back at Meyer's astonishing career, an extraordinary career that led him to make the cult classic *Beyond the Valley of the Dolls*.

Before his reign as the 'King of the Nudies', Meyer was a newsreel cameraman during World War II. Some of his footage appearing in *Patton* (1970). He used the skills he'd honed behind the camera to first shoot photos of James Dean on the set of *Giant* and then centrefold layouts for 'Playboy' before starting life as a director of softcore skin-flicks. His first film *The Immoral Mr. Teas* (1959) earned him his regal nickname and was a considerable success, leading to a succession of 'nudie cuties' during the early '60s including *Eve and the Handyman* (1961), *Erotica* (1961) and *Wild Gals of the Naked West* (1962).

Ever with his finger on the pulse of the American public's viewing proclivities, he realised that audiences would soon get bored of films with a

skimpy plot merely designed to expose naked flesh. His Gothic period followed, encompassing films like *Lorna* (1964), *Mudhoney* (1965), *Motorpsycho!* (1965) and *Faster, Pussycat! Kill! Kill!* (1965), the film that John Waters described as "beyond a doubt, the best movie ever made. It is possibly better than any film that will be made in the future."

All were shot in black and white and featured less nudity than his earlier films, but added gritty storylines and often brutal violence and inspired an era in sexploitation known as the 'roughies.' As a counterpoint, Meyer's breezy go-go dancing documentary *Mondo Topless* (1966) followed, before he worked on the melodrama *Common Law Cabin* (1967) and *Good Morning and... Goodbye!* (1967). Then, in 1968, came the film that changed everything for the director. *Vixen!* starring Erica Gavin, was a huge box-office draw, despite its 'X' rating. Critic Roger Ebert called the soft-core satire: "the quintessential Russ Meyer film" and Twentieth Century Fox stood up and took notice.

Richard D. Zanuck, the head of the studio, had seen *Vixen!* and was curious how much it cost. On hearing the film was made for around $70,000 and had taken home over $6 million, he exclaimed: "If he can get those production values for that kind of money, we need him on the team here." Meyer was given a three-picture deal, with each film granted a $1 million budget.

Fox had bought the rights to Jacqueline Susann's 1966 novel 'Valley of the Dolls'. The resulting adaptation, starring Barbara Parkins, Patty Duke and Sharon Tate, was a box-office smash despite reviews calling it "trashy, campy, soapy and melodramatic." A sequel to the tawdry tale of three pill-popping women trying to break into Hollywood was inevitable, and the project was given to Meyer.

"Neither of us had ever read the book, although I attempted to at one time," said *Beyond* scriptwriter Ebert, who became friends with Meyer after praising his work in an open letter to the 'Wall Street Journal'. "We did screen Mark Robson's film version of *Valley of the Dolls* before starting to write and this gave us the idea of making *Beyond the Valley of the Dolls* as a parody. We would take the basic situation and attempt to exaggerate it wildly."

And exaggerate they did! Ebert continued: "Nothing could be too outlandish, obvious, stereotyped, cliched, gaudy or extreme. The basic thrust behind *Beyond the Valley of the Dolls*, Meyer said more than once, was to leave the audience wondering what had hit it."

Beyond the Valley of the Dolls is a phantasmagorical delight which plays like a head-on collision between *Caligula* (1979), the Manson family, Roger Corman's *The Trip* (1967) and Josie and the Pussycats. This salacious slice of rock 'n' roll raunch follows Kelly MacNamara (Dolly Read), Casey Anderson (Cynthia Myers) and Petronella Danforth (Marcia McBroom), the three members of the rocking power trio The Kelly Affair. Managed by Kelly's

boyfriend Harris Allsworth (David Gurian), the band, with their unique take on psychedelic pop, is on the cusp of greatness. They fly to Los Angeles to find Kelly's estranged heiress aunt Susan Lake (Phyllis Davis) who, upon being reunited with her niece, promises Kelly a third of her inheritance.

Not everyone is so welcoming. Susan's lecherous financial advisor Porter Hall (Duncan McLeod) is intent on discrediting Kelly so he can bag the cash for himself. Susan, on the other hand, wants nothing but the best for her niece and introduces her and the band to rock producer Ronnie 'Z-Man' Barzell (John La Zar, in an incredible performance which channels legendary record producer Phil Spector) who seduces them with his salacious charm and promises of stardom. La Zar is given all the best dialogue ("You will drink the black sperm of my vengeance!") and a fine line in cravats. It's no exaggeration to call the swinging Svengali unforgettable. It's a shame he didn't follow through on his early promise as an actor.

Before you can say "This is my happening and it freaks me out", the girls are invited to one of the greatest parties ever committed to celluloid. Strawberry Alarm Clock perform *Incense and Peppermints* while a crazy collection of hot-to-trot partygoers jest like a spaced-out version of *The Muppet Show*'s *At the Dance* sketch. The groovy partygoers include Pam Grier, in her first ever on-screen appearance, Meyer regular Haji, *Super Vixens* star Charles Napier and the voracious Edy Williams - who married Meyer shortly after the film's release in 1970 - playing Ashley St. Ives ("You're a groovy boy. I'd like to strap you on sometime!") Mike Myers used the scene as a template for a soiree in *Austin Powers: International Man of Mystery* (1997).

Soon-to-be blaxploitation star Grier was McBroom's roommate at the time which is how she got the part. Despite her sole line of dialogue being cut, a photo of her in the first party scene was prominently featured in a 1970 'Playboy' layout on the film.

Following their impromptu performance of *Find It* at Z-Man's orgiastic bash, the renamed Carrie Nations are signed up by the crazed producer and the cautionary tale that follows warns any young band of the perils of wild sex, copious narcotics and signing up with a crazed androgynous megalomaniac who thinks he is Super Woman. Relationships are destroyed as the bond that ties the girls together is stretched to breaking point. Suicide, orgies, abortion, decapitation, fellatio with a handgun and

sexually confused superheroes follow, leaving the entire cast in meltdown.

In a finale that would make Mario Bava proud, Erica Gavin - who was introduced to Meyer by *Faster Pussycat Kill! Kill!* stars Tura Satana and Haji when they were working together at a strip club - is one of the victims of Z-Man's killing spree. Meyer and Ebert based the dark, twisted ending on the horrific Tate-LaBianca murders committed by Charles Manson's 'family' just a few months before Meyer began shooting *Beyond*. Cynthia Myers and singer Lynn Carey, who provided vocals for many of the film's memorable songs, had both dated Jay Sebring (one of the victims of that awful night) and Gavin also knew Sebring. The actress had gone to school with the LaBianca's daughter Susan, dated one of Manson's attorneys Paul J. Fitzgerald, and received letters from 'family' member Susan Atkins.

That connection to the real-life tragic events made the fact that the actress is murdered in *Beyond the Valley of the Dolls* even more difficult to watch. She explained in an interview in 'Glamour Girls': "The whole concept of

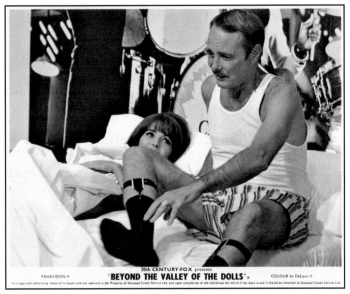

watching your head get blown off is scary. And having the gun in my mouth - it makes you wonder, what if something went wrong? Someone has referred to my gun fellatio scene as a classic example of cult film violence. It is, but it's very scary."

The film's ending is at odds with much of what had played out before. This was meant to be funny satire. "You create the greatest satire in the world if you direct everybody at right angles and don't say it's a comedy, just play everything straight. If you try to make it funny, it doesn't come off," Meyer told his biographer David K. Frasier decades later. "Two actors on *Dolls* understood - John La Zar and Michael Blodgett (who plays high-priced gigolo Lance Rocke)." As recalled in Jimmy McDonough's indispensable book 'Big Bosoms and Square Jaws', Charles Napier told Ebert: "You wrote this, Roger. It reads like a comedy to me. But, hell, Russ treats it like Eugene O'Neill."

Ever the provocateur, Meyer wanted to push boundaries in a mainstream setting. Ebert recalled on his website: "Because the movie was stuck with the X, Meyer wanted to re-edit certain scenes in order to include more nudity (he shot many scenes in both X and R versions). But the studio, still in the middle of a cash-flow crisis, wanted to rush the film into release. Meyer still waxes nostalgic for the "real" X version of *BVD*, which exists only in his memory but includes many much steamier scenes starring the movie's many astonishingly beautiful heroines and villainesses."

The soundtrack, especially the Carrie Nations fuzzed-out classics, saw industry legend Stu Phillips handle production duties as well as composing some of the songs. Bob Stone and Lynn Carey provided the lyrics. C.K. Strong member Carey and Barbara 'Sandi' Robison of The Peanut Butter Conspiracy provided the singing voices that made Read and Myers sound so good. "Talk on the street and reviews of my group were really good," Carey explained to 'Femme Fatale' magazine. "And I was this voluptuous blonde with this gigantic voice and Russ Meyer wanted somebody with a really big voice."

Beyond was a success at the box office despite being released in the UK as a double bill with *Myra Breckinridge*, the catastrophic adaptation of the Gore Vidal novel starring Mae West, John Huston and Raquel Welch. Not that all at Fox were happy. Grace Kelly, who was a member of the Fox board, was shocked that the director known as 'King Leer' was being financed by her studio. Luckily for her, Meyer's deal with Fox was terminated after his adaptation of Irving Wallace's 1969 novel 'The Seven Minutes' tanked at the box-office. Audiences were not ready to see a sexless Meyer courtroom drama with no nudity and Tom Selleck.

There was also a rumoured *Beyond* sequel in the works, but it never eventuated. Meyer and Ebert did reunite to work on the Sex Pistols movie *Who Killed Bambi?*, the film that would eventually become *The Great Rock 'n' Roll Swindle*. Legend has it that Rotten was a huge fan of *Beyond the Valley of the Dolls*. Only one shot was filmed for the Bambi sequence before financing fell through. The band's manager Malcolm McLaren said Fox pulled out after reading the screenplay. Ebert says: "This seems unlikely because the studio would not have green-lighted the film without reading the script." The writer also stated that Meyer said "McLaren had made false promises of financing and was broke. Electricians and others had walked off after not being paid. Meyer himself demanded each week's salary be deposited every Monday morning."

Back in 2011, David O. Russell was planning a Russ Meyer biopic, written by *Lovelace* screenwriter Merritt Johnson. That project never came to fruition but the story behind the making of this cult classic was going to be told *by Once* and *Sing Street* director John Carney. *Russ & Roger Go Beyond* was set to star Josh Gad as Roger Ebert and Will Ferrell as Meyer. Again, the project faltered, the filmmakers worried that a film about a larger-than-life sexploitation director would be a tone-deaf folly in the #MeToo era. The film's producer David Permut told 'The Playlist': "We had funding and were ready to make the movie. That green button turned into a red button literally overnight the moment the Harvey [Weinstein] news hit the world. "

What we do still have though is *Beyond the Valley of the Dolls* itself, the ultimate midnight movie, a remarkable snapshot of the "nightmare world of show business," that titillates and exhilarates in equal measure. It's

arguably Meyer's masterpiece, although *Faster, Pussycat! Kill! Kill!* aficionados would disagree.

There is no other film like *Beyond the Valley of the Dolls*. Once seen, it can never be forgotten.

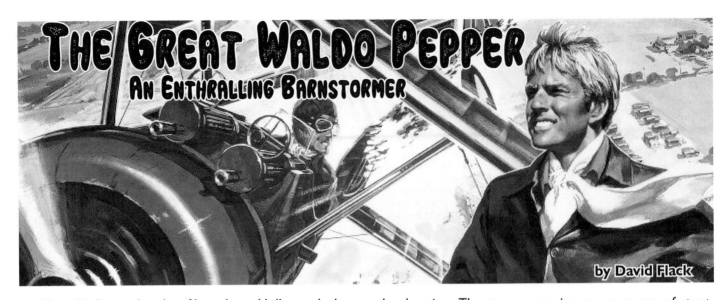

THE GREAT WALDO PEPPER
AN ENTHRALLING BARNSTORMER

by David Flack

When Hollywood makes films about Hollywood, they tend to include a large amount of humour and stunt work (e.g. *Nickelodeon, Hooper, The Stunt Man* etc.). *The Great Waldo Pepper* is another which ticks those boxes. Depicting barnstorming flying sequences and daredevil aerial stunts that are being filmed for action pictures in the mid '20s and early '30s, this enthralling and impressively made film is a good watch. It is directed by George Roy Hill who does a great job here, working with Robert Redford for the third and final time after *Butch Cassidy and the Sundance Kid* (1969) and *The Sting* (1973). Paul Newman had appeared with Redford in those two, but isn't involved in *Waldo Pepper* (though he nearly was, as I'll mention later). Hill and Newman would eventually reunite for one last time for the sport comedy-drama *Slap Shot* in 1977.

The plot follows an ex-pilot who, eight years after World War 1, takes up stunt flying and sets up a barnstorming show. He finds himself in a rivalry with another flyer (Bo Svenson). They eventually team up and develop a show which thrills crowds with increasingly daring and dangerous stunts. He also aims to meet up with his hero Ernst Kessler (Bo Brundin), a former German ace fighter pilot, and ends up filming air stunts for Hollywood movies in the 1930s.

The film has a great look and feel for its period and is done in the distinctive feel-good style that characterises many of George Roy Hill's movies. It grabs you from the opening moments and provides good, blustery entertainment for the duration. The story comprises many scenes of stunt flying and the preparation for them, but it really works largely thanks to two things: first, the likable performances from the whole cast, and second, the highly impressive flight scenes which look good even on a small screen and must have looked absolutely fantastic on a cinema screen. All the airborne stuff was done for real - no fancy effects, no studio back projection. At many points, I found myself thinking: "How the hell did they do that?" It's enormously impressive, and the film stands as a tribute to the stunt team and the technical crew who capture many eye-popping sequences. That said, as great as the technical stuff is it wouldn't be half as effective without good characterisation to go with it. And *The Great Waldo Pepper* delivers good characterisation in spades.

Though the film contains lots of humour and light-heartedness, there are at least two occasions where the tone is markedly bleak. Both generate a good quota of suspense and drama. One - possibly the best scene in the whole film - involves the inconsiderate, unthinking actions of a member of the crowd and results in a horrible tragedy. I find the sequence harrowing and disturbing, generating genuine anger and sadness.

It seems important not to discuss the events of the story in too much detail, because the less you know, the more you will enjoy it. Instead, I will focus on the performances, starting with Redford as the eponymous Waldo Pepper. As already mentioned, this was Redford's third film with director Hill and he gives a very assured, likable performance which oozes charm, confidence and vulnerability. From the opening scenes, we find ourselves charmed by him as he pimps his aerial adventure ride in a plane to the crowds. He obviously loves flying and has no problem enthralling the crowds with his patter, especially the ladies. There is an amusing early scene when he manages to get rid of a rival flyer who is out to steal his customers. For me, this is one of Redford's best performances and you're on his side every step of the way.

The supporting cast is vital to the film's success, and pretty much everyone is in winning form. The part of Axel Olsson, the rival flyer who Pepper teams up with, is played by Bo Svenson. Apparently, Paul Newman was considered for the role, which would have marked the third pairing of the stars with this director had it come to fruition. The cynic in me thinks that Newman might have read the script and realised that, unlike the two previous films, he would be playing a secondary character here. But it might just be that he saw that the main role as a great fit for Redford's talents and simply wasn't interested in a supporting role. Personally, I'm glad he didn't take the role of Olsson - it would have been a different film with two big stars sharing the limelight, probably not as good. Svenson gives the best performance of his career, in his first big-screen film. Previously, he had been toiling away in guest roles in various TV shows dating back to 1965. He was normally a one-note, rather grouchy actor, perhaps best known for taking over Joe Don Baker's role in two inferior *Walking Tall* sequels and a short-lived 1981 TV series. For a while, he was the highest paid TV actor in America. He was notable for his height (well over 6 feet) which gave him an imposing if somewhat awkward look. He's very good in *The Great Waldo Pepper*, demonstrating a fine rapport with Redford. In the early scenes, his Swedish accent is somewhat wobbly, coming and going until it eventually disappears altogether. In these early moments, he sounds rather like Arnold Schwarzenegger in one of his light-hearted modes. His character, like Redford's, shows a vulnerability that adds to his charm. All in all, it's a good, underrated performance.

Bo Brundin is also effective as Ernst Kessler, the former German fighter ace from World War 1 who is Pepper's hero and inspiration. He doesn't appear much until the later part of the film, but manages to convey the sense that his character has outlived his time after the war and wishes he'd died in combat like many of his comrades and opponents. It's a lovely, world-weary performance. Brundin fluctuated between film and TV for the rest of his career, and passed away in 2022 at the age of 85.

Edward Herrmann also impresses as plane designer Ezra Stiles who becomes frustrated when his ambitions are stalled due to Pepper being banned from flying. Ezra decides to fly himself while Waldo is grounded, with

tragic consequences. The scene really disturbs the viewer and lingers in the mind. It is suspenseful and ultimately horrifying, and very well played by Herrmann and Redford. The actor had appeared with Redford a year earlier in *The Great Gatsby*, and enjoyed a good run of film and TV appearances before passing away in 2014.

Geoffrey Lewis adds another fine supporting performance to his long list as Newt, Pepper's former squadron leader, now a lawyer who works for the aviation association and is assigned to make sure Pepper does not thwart the law when he is banned from flying. Newt has a lot of respect for Pepper, and vice versa, but is determined to do his job to the letter. Lewis was a very underrated character-actor, and he's in good form here, especially in his final scene. He is best known for a number of supporting roles in Clint Eastwood films, and his chillingly memorable vampire-in-a-rocking-chair in Tobe Hooper's excellent *Salem's Lot* (1979). Lewis passed away in 2015.

There are two significant female roles. Susan Sarandon plays Mary Beth, a waitress who knows Axel and sees an opportunity to make something of herself by joining him and Pepper in their stunt show. She takes up wing-walking, which turns out not to be a good career move for them, especially her. This was early in her screen career, and in the same year she would appear in one of her signature roles in *The Rocky Horror Picture Show*. Her part here isn't particularly big, but it's important to the plot and she makes a strong impression. She went on, of course, to enjoy a distinguished career which included the likes of *Thelma and Louise* (1991) and *Dead Man Walking* (1995), amongst many others.

The other female role, Maude, is played by Margot Kidder. Maude is presented as a kind of on-and-off romantic interest for Waldo. She obviously loves him, but is resigned to the fact that she will always come second to his aerial exploits. It's not a large role, but Kidder makes something of it, showing herself to be a talented actress. She was a bigger name than Sarandon at the time, having just come off *Black Christmas* (1974) and what was arguably her career-best role in Brian De Palma's *Sisters*

(1972). She had a good, interesting career which peaked when she portrayed Lois Lane in several of the Superman films. In her later years, she struggled with her mental health and committed suicide in 2018.

I should reserve a special mention to Philip Bruns who very nearly steals the film in an amusing performance as Bob Dillhoefer, the entrepreneur who runs the flying show that Waldo eventually joins. Bruns, like most of the cast, acted mostly in TV, though he did appear in the similar *The Stunt Man* (1980). He passed away in 2012.

All in all, *The Great Waldo Pepper* is a rip-roaring, hugely entertaining film that delivers for the most part. Only the climatic showdown between Pepper and Kessler disappoints somewhat. It starts well enough, as if two knights are jousting, but seems rushed and doesn't play out as effectively as it might have. The rather inconclusive finish to their duel leaves things up in the air (excuse the pun).

For this review, I rewatched the film for only the third time. It was hugely enjoyable, one of those films that gets better every time I see it. The time flew by (another pun, sorry). It has an abundance of winning performances and leaves you with a sense of awe. A fine movie that I plan to revisit again in the near future.

66

Hello to the Cynical Seventies, "GOODBYE GEMINI"

by Simon J. Ballard

When Jennie Hall wrote her novel 'Ask Agamemnon' in 1964, telling of young siblings Jacki and Julian's naïve embrace of London, there was an air of optimism in Britain. The land may have been pock-marked by bomb damage from the Blitz, but New Towns such as Milton Keynes were on the way and London's skyline offered a taste of the future with the completion of the Post Office Tower. Meanwhile, as *Top of the Pops* first aired on the BBC, pirate radio stations offered the latest chart hits and The Beatles starred in their film *A Hard Day's Night*.

By the time the movie adaptation was released in 1970, the fresh, clean concrete was stained and cracked, Paul McCartney announced he was leaving the band, and Mick Jagger was fined £200 for possession of cannabis. The end of the '60s had ended with the Charles Manson killings, thus ending the hippie dream as nihilism replaced free love. The ever-widening cynicism built on the countercultural movement of the '60s instilled in the youth of the day a healthy disdain toward the high and mighty they no longer had any respect for.

Not that any of this bothers our twin protagonists, played by Judy Geeson and Martin Potter. They have decided to visit London on their spring break. London will be exciting, and with father away in Mexico on business, they can be themselves, by themselves. Won't that be fun?

This is a Peter Snell production, and like *The Wicker Man* to come, here we see two worlds collide, two sets of beliefs and behaviour patterns utterly at odds with each other. This is roundly realised by the fresh direction of youthful Canadian director Alan Gibson, a year or so away from giving Hammer's Dracula a kick to the 20th century.

The opening sequence points towards the state the decade would soon descend into. As the twins look out the window with childlike joy, the camera tracks away from a peeling billboard, neatly emphasising their naïve enthusiasm against the faded splendour of reality as they approach the Westway system, much resented by the local populace. This is played out to the rather jaunty and very modern song *Tell the World We're Not In* by The Peddlers. The soundtrack is gorgeous throughout.

Goodbye Gemini, released in Britain on 6th August 1970, is a movie that captures perfectly a sociological ill of the time - as the Establishment would have it - the permissive society. With the advent of the pill in 1967, and apparently encouraged by Woodstock, the youth of the day felt emboldened to exchange freely in carnal desires left, right and centre with gay abandonment. And gay liberation too, what with the decriminalisation of homosexuality the same year women were given freedom of choice. These were heady days indeed as the conservative-minded faced a war with the counterculture brigade. And this feature is a perfect snapshot of that time, almost approaching a mondo documentary style in places.

Fellow novelist Edmund Ward was tasked with bringing Hall's book to script. His own book 'Summer in Retreat' had won the Author's Club Award in 1957 and tells of a Bohemian coming home to settle down, and in many ways, *Goodbye Gemini* takes the opposite route, with the cosseted, entitled twins seeking new adventures and in the process landing themselves way out of depth amid the modern London scene.

Though achingly contemporary at the time, the story

67

- as in the novel - is essentially a Greek tragedy as Jacki and Julian's lives spiral way out of control. Essentially, the plot is one that extrapolates Jacki and Julian's childlike minds and attitudes and allows one man to manipulate this to his own ends, at the same time not realising that an infantile approach to life can be deadly to others. This is Clive, performed with some gusto and intensity by Alexis Kanner, with a pair of outrageous and almost horizontal sideboards. This is a man who exudes the off-kilter zeitgeist of the time, having played a key role in the last episode of *The Prisoner* after an earlier appearance, and as a man who explores all the nightlife Soho has to offer in the 1969 short *Twenty-Nine*. He is captivating to watch, almost operatic in his movements.

Along with Agamemnon, Jacki and Julian meet with Clive and Denise, a reluctant prostitute, at the Royal Vauxhall Tavern, south London's oldest gay pub where many a cabaret act takes place to this day. This scene really is a snapshot of the London clubbing scene as we witness a drag act strip show and it exudes an authenticity sadly lacking from the crashed party of *Dracula AD 1972*.

Incidentally, the same act appears in the same year's *The Secret of Dorian Gray*!

Clive takes the twins to a party on a houseboat, tastefully decorated in white and red - the pure and bloody, very apt. Here, we get to know his dodgy and slimy nature through his associates who include the languid lounge lizard David, played just on the right side of camp by Freddie Jones, who seems to be having the time of his life as he reclines on a hammock while sipping drinks and slipping out barbed comments to Clive. He idly drops into the conversation that a man is after Clive for money, wishing with a glint in his eye that some harm will come to him. This is self-centred decadence, a growing '70s trait, impure and simple.

The twins themselves come under much scrutiny from their fellow partygoers, their freshness and innocence marking them out as something of a novelty. Especially intrigued is MP James Harrington-Smith, who remarks later: "They carry their own universe with them." This was one of the last roles for Michael Redgrave who was suffering early-onset Parkinson's Disease. It's a measured,

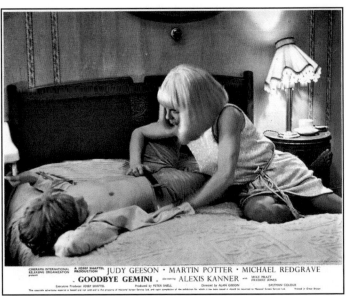

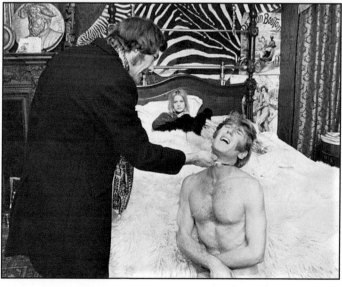

dignified performance with a calmness against the storm and tempest about to envelop the character. After the Profumo scandal, the sight of a politician enjoying the egregiousness of a party where anything goes wouldn't have seemed that shocking at the time, especially when shows and publications like *That Was the Week That Was* and 'Private Eye' reminded us just how human and fallible such exalted figures behaved, to put it mildly.

Clive and Denise soon make a nest within the vast rooms of the Twin's inherited house, Clive especially taking advantage of the situation despite the open hostility and jealousy of Julian. Jacki herself is only semi-inviting, as a means to distance herself from her brother's brooding sexual attraction. This incestuous aspect was far more blatant than that seen in the novel.

This is what they do with equanimity; using others with neither shame nor adult supervision to hinder them - "Spoilt, immature, and vicious" is how Denise sums up Julian shortly before he gives her a slap. It's an explosive combination when one takes Clive into account, a powder-keg situation, redolent of that spirit of living for today and sod tomorrow that would summarise the '70s as weed became acid and the summer of love became the winter of discontent.

With Mike Pratt's rather nasty turn as gangster Rob Barstowe after his £400, Clive is in it right up to his sideburns, and in consequence offers Julian a sight of London he was not expecting as they repair to the seedy Woodlands Hotel and a night with two guys in drag who proceed to rape Julian. The scene cuts away from the actual act but is redolent of menace and expectant dread. All in the aid of blackmail as photos of the degrading act are presented to a naturally horrified Julian, whom we saw earlier in a nervous state in front of his sister, unable to face his own reflection in the mirror. This nasty, predatory portrayal of gay men in drag cropped up two years later in an early episode of Amsterdam-based crime show *Van der Valk*. For alternate lifestyle, read danger - sadly all too common in this period.

When Jacki gets wind of Clive's scheme, there is a nice use of the zoom lens Gibson would make free with in his modern Hammer Dracula productions as the camera focusses on the twin's twin image in the mirror, a look of satisfaction shared as though by telepathic link a plot of their own has just hatched.

Cue a rather heightened and almost baroque scene as the twins dare Clive to be able to tell them apart. Once his blindfold is removed, he is sat in front of a mirror as they stand either side of him, draped in white sheets with only their eyes visible. Clive's uncertainty as to what is going on is short lived as two ceremonial Japanese swords are thrust into his neck as Agamemnon watches on. It was all a game, and the nasty man has been dealt a lesson. The sight of Clive's terrified image reflected in the blade of the sword is nice and stylish, and rather similar to a shot Edgar Wright achieved in *Last Night in Soho*, another movie about hopes for London turning sour.

There then follows a rather jarring cut as we see Jacki fleeing across a bridge, only to be picked up by a passing James. I say this with no criticism, for it neatly replicates the unsettled and disjointed nature of Jacki who has gone into immediate amnesiac shock, as though her childish mind cannot cope with the extremely adult act committed. As James leads her away from the wharfside, I rather like the tangle of barbed wire that comes into focus.

The sensitivity of Redgrave's James forms a neat contrast to the jangled and disturbed condition of Jacki, and it is here the paternal compassion of the MP comes to the surface, though this may only be due to circumstances rather than instinct! Indeed, they are seen to share a bed in all (frustrated?) innocence at one point.

As Jacki's memory returns in fragments, she goes back to the house via taxi, tripping over the body of Clive, and only emitting a scream at the sight of Agamemnon who has been torn to shreds. This alerts the attention of Brian Wilde's pipe-smoking cabbie (!) and prompts a search for the twins. One really feels the net tightening, and a grim sense of inevitable doom for this seems to be a situation that playing games will do nothing to alleviate.

True enough, as more pieces return to her, Jacki remembers Clive mentioning the hotel he took Julian to, and this is where she finds her brother - symbiotically wearing black as she is - though in a horribly dishevelled condition, both in mind and body. A shilling for the gas metre will provide only temporary warmth...

Alan Gibson, fresh from the rather excruciating Hammer thriller *Crescendo*, allows the full might of his creative juices to flow freely here, and offers up several symbolic elements revolving around reflections of dual imagery. A close up of a mirror cuts to Julian cleaning a pair of glasses shortly before they plot the death of the severe housekeeper with the strategic placing of teddy bear Agamemnon at the top of the stairs. Later, in a state of desperation, we see Jacki wandering around a market, with reflective puddles and a pair of caged budgies foregrounded. *Goodbye Gemini* is populated by such flourishes throughout.

Like his later score for Hammer's *Hands of the Ripper*, Christopher Gunning laces the proceedings with romantic yet tragic music, bringing out the twin's sense of helplessness against the tides of adulthood, and join their performances in seeking our sympathies for the pair despite their murderous act upon the housekeeper. As for Clive, well, he dared to play in their den.

We are never privy to Jacki and Julian's background regarding their upbringing, but one gets a sense of arrested development where the normal rules of responsibility and compassion have become muddled. Their freedom is their destruction, and that to me speaks of horror, a genre this film can either sit in or out, depending on your judgement. For me, it's a case of *Goodbye Gemini*, you're it.

You'll feel four hands reaching for you— when the **GEMINI TWINS! Arrive!**

CINERAMA RELEASING presents A JOSEPH SHAFTEL PRODUCTION starring

JUDY GEESON · MARTIN POTTER · ALEXIS KANNER MICHAEL REDGRAVE

"GOODBYE GEMINI"

MIKE PRATT · FREDDIE JONES · EDMUND WARD · screenplay by Ask Agamemnon by JENNI HALL · executive producer JOSEF SHAFTEL

produced by PETER SNELL · directed by ALAN GIBSON · FROM CINERAMA RELEASING COLOR [R]

ASSAULT ON PRECINCT 13

A BLOOD OATH OF VENGEANCE

by Kev Hurst

Napoleon Wilson: Still have the gun?
Leigh: Two shots. Should I save them for the two of us?
Napoleon Wilson: Save 'em for the first two assholes who come through that vent.

Two years after his directorial debut *Dark Star* in 1974, independent filmmaker and talented writer John Carpenter released the suspenseful, volatile siege-themed pseudo-horror *Assault on Precinct 13*. It marked the start of a great period for Carpenter. Two years later, he would terrify the world with *Halloween*, his tale of a disturbed child-man who goes on a murderous rampage. Alongside Mario Bava's *A Bay of Blood* (1971) and Bob Clark's *Black Christmas* (1974), it pretty much invented the template for the popular slasher sub-genre. He followed it with the likes of *The Fog* (1980), *Escape from New York* (1981), *The Thing* (1982), *Christine* (1983) and *Big Trouble in Little China* (1986).

Assault on Precinct 13 remains as fresh today as it was the day it was released nearly half a century ago. It laid the groundwork for most of what Carpenter did afterwards, showing him to be a budding auteur who hinged his stories upon paranoia, claustrophobia and existential panic. He showed a knack for presenting cool lead characters too, blue-collar everyman heroes. Three

of these were portrayed by Kurt Russell (Snake Plissken in *Escape From New York*, MacReady in *The Thing* and, my personal favourite, Jack Burton in *Big Trouble in Little China*). Carpenter's talent didn't end there - he was also a gifted musician, often composing ominous synth-wave scores for his own films.

It's no exaggeration to call Carpenter a master of horror, comparable to the likes of David Cronenberg, Tobe Hooper, Wes Craven and George A. Romero. The movies he made in the '70s and '80s were extraordinary. And the run began with *Assault on Precinct 13*.

Carpenter made the film soon after his 16mm science-fiction parody *Dark Star*, which was ultra-low-budget and grew out of a student project. Even in its expanded form, *Dark Star* has an almost student film feel about it. Despite boasting the tagline 'The ultimate cosmic comedy!', I must admit I've always found it a slog to get through. I don't find it at all humorous, and nowadays I look upon it chiefly as a curio, a chance to see where this celebrated cult filmmaker cut his teeth. In the aftermath of *Dark Star*, Carpenter wasn't exactly inundated with directorial offers so he became a sort of 'gun for hire', writing a couple of screenplays to keep his feet in the door. He sold one to Columbia which later became *The Eyes of Laura Mars* (made and released in 1978). The other, initially titled *The*

Anderson Alamo, would become *Assault on Precinct 13*.

With the help of friends from his days at the University of Southern California and private investors, Carpenter raised a meagre $100,000 to make the film. If we agree that *Dark Star* is student-level stuff, then *Assault* should be looked upon as Carpenter's first really cinematic piece of moviemaking. He made it by his rules, retaining full control over all aspects of the production. There was no interference from outside presences. He strips the story down to the bare essentials. There are hardly any special effects (he'd tried that with *Dark Star*), no big names in the cast and crew, and the narrative is very singular and straightforward. This directness is no bad thing in terms of storytelling - too many movies are undone by being overly elaborate, intricate or sophisticated. *Assault on Precinct 13* does not fall into that trap.

The story gets underway when a father is traumatised after witnessing his daughter heartlessly murdered by a leader of a multi-racial gang known as Street Thunder. The gangsters are seeking vengeance for the mass murder of some of their acquaintances at the hands of the police the night before. The distraught father hunts down the gang and gains some partial retribution by gunning dead one of the four main leaders. But this only causes the other three gang warlords to become more inflamed with rage, and the father is forced to take sanctuary at a nearby police station. The soon-to-be-closed station, Precinct 13, is operating with a skeleton crew consisting of duty officer Ethan Bishop (Austin Stoker) who is on his first day and new to the team, female station secretaries Leigh (Laurie Zimmer) and Julie (Nancy Loomis), and one sergeant, Chaney (Henry Brandon). The justifiably upset father tells them what he has done, and while he is having his breakdown the gang begins to lay siege to the police station. With the building in the process of being shut down, it's unlikely any help will arrive any time soon.

Before the siege gets underway, we are introduced to the anti-hero of the story, Napoleon Wilson (Darwin Joston), a convict being transferred along with two other inmates to a state penitentiary. The prison bus transporting them is forced to make an unplanned stop at Precinct 13 for

medical supplies after one of the convicts falls seriously ill. Napoleon and co. soon find themselves fighting for survival with the rest of the station crew as an endless wave of gang members lays siege to the building.

It is well known that *Assault on Precinct 13* borrows narrative aspects from *Rio Bravo* (1959). Carpenter considered Howard Hawks (who helmed *Rio Bravo*) one of the most inspirational filmmakers of all time. He would later remake *The Thing from Another World* (1951) - also directed by Hawks - as *The Thing* in 1982. Carpenter also derives strong similarities of mood and tone from George A. Romero's *Night of the Living Dead* (1968). That film had a small group holed up in farmhouse close to a cemetery fighting off waves of marauding zombies; this one relocates a very similar narrative to a small police station in a Los Angeles ghetto. The gang themselves may have human faces, but they're like modern zombies. As we watch limitless gang members being gunned down while attacking the police station, we're reminded of the zombie hordes being gunned down in Romero's *Night of the Living Dead*. Romero's film opens in broad daylight with siblings visiting their father's grave and sighting the first zombie. It approaches and attacks them, forcing the lead character Barbara to take shelter in a nearby farmhouse. Carpenter's *Assault on Precinct 13* also opens in daylight with a frightened character taking shelter in a nearly deserted police station. Carpenter also borrows certain character elements from *Night of the Living Dead* such as the trusting bond which develops between black character Bishop and white character Leigh, a direct reference to Ben and Barbara's relationship in *NOTLD*.

Assault on Precinct 13 never really has a dull moment. The pacing is excellent. With a runtime in the region of 90 minutes, there is no tedious filler at all. The story is accompanied by an on-screen clock which appears periodically to keep us abreast of the chronology of events - the Saturday 3.10am shootings, Bishop starting his work shift at 4.50pm, Napoleon being prepared for his transfer from jail at 5.11pm, etc. This really helps us to form a sense of time and space, as well as linking the connecting plot lines. We meet the lead characters within a small amount of time; their backstories are kept minimal and relevant so that it's full steam ahead as soon as the siege narrative kicks in. In later films, Carpenter would come back to the idea of putting a small focus group in a perilous situation - *Halloween* has high school student Laurie Strode and her friends stalked by a maniac; *The Fog* shows a handful of residents residing in the coastal town of Antonio Bay being menaced by supernatural forces; *The Thing* gives us the crew of an Antarctic research station threatened by an alien; *Prince of Darkness* pits a small team of researchers against the agents of Satan; *They Live*

presents Nada, a lone drifter, trying to save mankind from subliminal aliens; and *Ghosts of Mars* is virtually a carbon facsimile of *Assault on Precinct 13* relocated to space.

The characters from *Assault on Precinct 13* may have minimal backstories, but they're still interesting and well-layered, with genuine personality and soul. I think Carpenter displayed a knack for writing terrific characters at this point in in his career. I noted earlier that his favourite filmmaker was Howard Hawks, and you can see Hawks' influence in the way he writes. The anti-hero Napoleon Wilson could have stepped right out of a Hawks movie - he is a clear precursor to the likes of Snake Plissken from *Escape From New York*. His anti-authoritarian characteristics and mannerisms are a reflection of the classic Hawksian cowboy caricature, right down to the line "got a smoke?" which he utters numerous times throughout. Wilson is essentially an old gunslinger thrown into a modern urban environment. Hawks also liked to show female characters who were the equal of their male counterparts, and in *Assault* we have Leigh, a strong, tough-talking woman who retains her femininity while always speaking her mind. Carpenter would use strong women in the likes of *Halloween*, *The Fog*, *Starman* and *Ghosts of Mars*.

Throughout *Assault on Precinct 13*, there is no break in the intensity of the situation; the threat is always severe and those at risk face near impossible odds of survival. One by one, the crew of the station are killed until, by the end, only Bishop, Wilson and Leigh remain to fend off the army of near-supernatural hoodlums who keep coming at them, relentlessly exacting their vengeance.

I've always adored the sound design and scoring in Carpenter's films. He excels at creating mood and atmosphere, and in some of his movies the theme music is as iconic as the movie itself. This is the case with *Assault on Precinct 13*. First heard over the title screen with its blood-red colour credits, the score starts with a drum machine, almost hinting at some kind of futuristic setting, then the synth bass kicks in and the main theme begins. An

important point to make is that there is a synth lead part in the background playing a discordant E-flat note (not diatonic). This note is sometimes referred to as a tritone (or a *diabolus in musica* - "the devil in music") and is used to signify evil/danger, etc. The rest of the theme is diatonic (in key), with an occasional suspended G chord (C is played over this chord to add suspense.) The tritone in the opening theme is used subtly during certain scenes at the beginning of the film, like when the gang are in their hideout listening to a news report about the stolen weapons. The single note is held and becomes more prominent, getting louder, during the infamous blood oath scene in which the four warlords cut their own arms and let their blood dribble into a pot. The scoring adds depth to the gruesome on-screen ritual that is taking place.

Carpenter has never been entirely popular within mainstream Hollywood. Despite its failure at the box office, *Assault on Precinct 13* has over the years gained huge popularity and a devoted following. Carpenter has said on numerous occasions that it was his most fun he had on a film set. It's a masterwork of low-budget filmmaking, proving that a big budget isn't needed when a confident and innovative director is at the helm. The idea that less can be more, that something incredible can be done on a shoestring budget, is barely recognised in the current cinematic climate.

Assault on Precinct 13 touches on themes of gun violence, racism, gang culture and vigilante justice, but first and foremost it provides a whole load of suspenseful entertainment for its duration. There was a remake in 2005 staring Ethan Hawke and Laurence Fishburne, but it didn't perform brilliantly at the box office and now resides in the pantheon of unwanted remakes that nobody asked for.

The original sits perfectly among other urban thrillers of the time like *Death Wish* (1974) and *The Warriors* (1979). Come to think of it, if you were to view the three of them back-to-back, you'd be in for one hell of a good night!

A cop with
a war on his hands.
His enemy...
an army of street killers.
His only ally...
a convicted
murderer.

ASSAULT
ON PRECINCT 13

A FILM BY JOHN CARPENTER

John Carpenter's "ASSAULT ON PRECINCT 13"
starring Austin Stoker, Darwin Joston, Laurie Zimmer.
C.K.K. Productions Producer J. S. KAPLAN. Screenplay and Music JOHN CARPENTER.
Photography DOUGLAS KNAPP. Editor JOHN T. CHANCE. Sound WILLIAM COOPER.
Panavision   Metrocolor   Hoyts Distribution

MASTERPIECE OR MIS-STEP?

by Martin Dallard

Right from the outset, there's no mistaking that *1941* is a comedy. In the very first scene, director Steven Spielberg lampoons his own 1975 summer blockbuster *Jaws*, the film that made him a household name. The directing wunderkind makes it clear from the word go that nothing is off limits in this anarchic comic spectacle.

Spielberg was still, relatively speaking, the new kid on the block when *1941* was released. He'd started in television on such shows as *Columbo* and *Owen Marshall, Counselor at Law*. The TV-movie *Duel* raised his profile and he soon moved to the big screen with the low-budget classic *The Sugarland Express*, before hitting remarkable heights with the film adaptation of Peter Benchley's novel 'Jaws'. At the time, *Jaws* rewrote box-office records until it was ousted from the top spot in 1977 by a small indie film called *Star Wars*.

Spielberg followed his fishy tale with a suspenseful, well-oiled movie that dealt with aliens visiting this blue marble of ours, *Close Encounters of the Third Kind* (1977). That too was box office dynamite, and it was beginning to look like he could turn his hand to any celluloid genre and hit a home run. Alas, his next film would prove that wasn't necessarily the case.

Let's cast our beady eye at his 1979 entry, the slapstick comedy shtick that was *1941*. At the time, it received a lot of flak for failing to put huge numbers of bums on seats like his two previous outings. Despite the quality talent in front of the camera, despite the screenplay by Robert Zemeckis and Bob Gale (who would collaborate a few years later on a certain hit time travel movie), despite beautiful cinematography by William A. Fraker and despite a musical score by legendary composer John Williams, *1941* struggled to excite audiences. And this, it has to be said, lies squarely at the feet of Spielberg himself. With all this talent at his disposal and a lavish budget to throw at the project, you have to wonder what went wrong.

The film takes place a week after the bombing of Pearl Harbour. Hysteria sweeps the United States like toxic gas, and word on the street is that California is next on the target list of the Japanese forces. US Defence forces are mobilised to protect the nation and restore order before it all goes to hell in a handbag. In the meantime, the crew of a rogue Japanese submarine surface off the coast of California with one mission in mind: to wipe Hollywood off the map.

Although mobilised, the armed US forces are oblivious to the enemy sitting just off shore. It looks like Uncle Sam has been caught with his breeches down.

But the nefarious submarine commander (Toshiro Mifune) hasn't reckoned on Air Force pilot Captain Kelso (John Belushi) - Wild Bill to his friends - who patrols the skies in his busted-up P-40K Tomahawk. The only thing more busted-up than his plane is the good captain himself. Can Kelso's skewed sense of heroic nationalism save the day? Well, it's Belushi... what do you think?!?

When *Raiders of the Lost Ark* came out two years after *1941*, the "voiceover man" on the *Raiders* trailer didn't proudly state: "From the maker of *1941*..." Oh, he mentioned *Jaws* and *Close Encounters*, all right. But *1941*, Spielberg's most recent movie, didn't get mentioned at all. Now, doesn't that tell you something?

Those two home runs, *Jaws* and *Close Encounters*, had come one after the other. When *1941* didn't enjoy the same sort of commercial and critical success, it felt like certain factions in Hollywood were ebullient at the realisation that even Spielberg was capable of misfiring creatively. He *was* human and fallible, after all; he didn't in fact walk on water! But here's the rub - *1941* still picked up three Oscar nominations and made a profit (nowhere near as much as expected) for Universal and Columbia, who'd co-financed and distributed the picture.

Today, Spielberg seems perplexed that the film gets little appreciation in the US yet is looked on more favourably in Europe. He rationalises that it was too ahead of its time and would probably fare better with audiences if it were released today. That's certainly a claim for conjecture.

The origins of the project came about thanks to the two Bobs - Gale and Zemeckis - who were fresh out of film school, hawking around ideas and scripts to any studio that would listen. Eventually they hooked up with producer John Milius, who was willing to give them an opportunity since they'd graduated from the same school as him. One of their screenplays was called *Tank*, and although this wasn't picked up, it was the springboard for the war film that followed.

Milius, Gale and Zemeckis eventually settled on a rudimentary idea of what to do and gave their project the working title *The Night the Japs Attacked!* The two Bobs then scuttled off to immerse themselves in '40s Americana, to "get in the zone" to write their war epic. As they were turning over rocks for ideas, they stumbled upon an incident from February 1942 (two months after the attack on Pearl Harbour) where Los Angeles had believed itself to be under air attack by the Japanese. All power to the city was shut off and gun battery emplacements in the area spent a manic five minutes firing wildly into the night sky at... well, nothing as it turned out. Gale and Zemeckis knew they could use this real-life occurrence and blow it out of proportion for the film they had in mind. So, in a loose sense, the premise of *1941* was based on true events.

As for the Japanese submarine surfacing off the coast of California, it seems that too was loosely based on a true incident. In fact, the whole film is a smorgasbord of questionable real-life occurrences during the hysteria of the early day of America entering World War II. The Zoot Suit riots of the '40s also provided the inspiration for segments of the film. The riots occurred in 1943, when American sailors on leave were attacked by Mexican-American 'zoot-suiters' (style-conscious dancers whose look was popularised by performers like Cab Calloway). The skirmish led to further outbreaks of violence between

the armed forces, police and the zoot-suiters across the country. The authorities judged the outlandish zoot-suit outfits as an affront to the servicemen who were fighting to make America and the world safe again. These riots and the tension they aroused were added to the plot for the dance club punch-up, and the huge bust-up involving almost all the characters near the end of the picture.

With the script eventually knocked into shape, producer Milius showed it to his friend Steven Spielberg. Upon reading it, Spielberg saw it as an opportunity to let loose, to take the handbrake off and have some anarchic fun unlike his usual conservative style. When *1941* came to Spielberg's desk, preproduction was already well under way on *Close Encounters of the Third Kind* (a project that had real personal depth for the director) so he put the war epic aside for a while. Once *Close Encounters* was in the can, he had a year free and decided it was time to make the leap into outright farce and anarchy. From the outset, he didn't like the proposed title *The Night the Japs Attacked!*, considering it too abrasive.

Rewrites were being done all the time, many at the request of the director while he was still filming the Mothership scenes for *Close Encounters*. The ever-evolving script of *1941* ended up being something of a melting pot

for all involved. Nothing was off limits, and zany idea was piled upon zany idea. Bob Zemeckis admitted they threw in everything including "the kitchen sink!"

There's an old adage that too many cooks spoil the broth. That rings all too true with *1941*, the main problem being its glaring imbalances in tone and style. Everything seems off-kilter, and at times it's confusing following what's going on, or at least where the focus lies. That said, Spielberg's usual visual inventiveness is there in abundance (and, let's face it, there are few directors who can better him in that department). The jitterbug sequence in the club is incredibly frenetic, one of the standout scenes of the film, and you have to wonder why he took so long to dip his toe in the musical genre again with his remake of *West Side Story*. (Kate Capshaw's grand opening routine from *Indiana Jones and the Temple of Doom* [1984] would also show his clear love for, and skill at, putting together amazing musical sequences). Alas, the pacing and editing in *1941* are choppy. At least William Fraker's cinematography gives it a real sense of Americana, the old apple pie and white picket fencing of Norman Rockwell-style paintings shot through a gauze of nostalgia, depicting an authentic look for the age. Whatever you might criticise it for, you can't deny *1941* is beautiful to behold.

The production values are second to none, with model scenes depicting many outlandish action set pieces. The model work contributed to the budget ballooning out of control, but the results can clearly be seen on screen. One

thing you can say about Spielberg: he always gives his audiences bang for their buck.

Zemeckis and Gale were new to the game back then, and their future projects seem to be handled with greater comic flair and panache than this. Was *1941* their learning curve? It seems uncharacteristically unsubtle by their standards, though that might be due to the insistence of the director and producer.

Though flawed, *1941* shows an exuberance Spielberg hadn't demonstrated before. The man is having fun, which is blatantly obvious. *Jaws* actor Susan Backlinie returns for the film's opening scene, skinny dipping not off the shore of Amity Island but off California. She falls victim not to a 25-foot Great White shark but to Toshiro Mifune's surfacing submarine. It's an opening which serves as a giant wink to the viewer.

The cast on paper reads like a director's dream: Dan Aykroyd, Treat Williams, Slim Pickens, Nancy Allen, John Candy, Lorraine Gary, Toshiro Mifune, Robert Stack, Ned Beatty, John Belushi, Warren Oates and Christopher Lee (even James Caan is there, in an uncredited cameo as a sailor in the bar fight).

Relative newcomer Bobby Di Cicco gets one of the biggest roles, playing Wally Stephens, a greasy spoon worker who wants to get to the dance club and win back his old girlfriend. It was originally intended that Wally would be the focal character in the story, and that his story arc would touch (however briefly) each of the various plot points of the film. He would bind the sprawling narrative into a cohesive whole. However, this was either lost in the editing suite or fell victim to script changes along the way. Probably a bit of both. An extended cut of the film has been released in recent times which apparently attempts to improve some of the mistakes of the theatrical cut, but at this present time I lack the strength to watch it!

Casting Belushi as madcap pilot Kelso threw a spanner in the works, further unbalancing the out-of-control proceedings. Kelso was meant to be a tertiary character who appeared toward the end of the original script. When Belushi became attached to the role, both director and producer wanted to maximise the comic actor's timely

inventiveness so lengthened his scenes. The concept of "less is more" did not apply in this instance, especially since Belushi carried such comic clout. But with an unpredictable talent like Belushi so prominently involved, Spielberg soon found himself driving with the brakes cut.

The standout performance in the picture comes from Robert Stack, playing Major General Joseph W. Stilwell, a fictionalised version of a real life general whose level-headed outlook at such insanity seems itself almost insane. Regardless of the chaos reigning supreme, the general just wishes to sit in a darkened movie theatre for a couple of hours to watch *Dumbo*! He sums the whole picture up neatly in a single sentence after briefly bumping into Kelso near the film's end. Watching the crazed pilot manically disappear into the darkness, Stilwell utters: "That is the craziest son of a bitch I ever saw!"

The role of Stilwell was originally offered to John Wayne, but the Duke turned it down on grounds of the project being anti-American, in spite of Spielberg trying to explain it was a farce.

There's a vast amount of top-drawer talent in the picture, but few are utilised to their true potential which is a genuine shame. The two actors who seem to play well off each other are Mifune's Commander Mitamura and Lee's German U-boat Captain, Wolfgang von Kleinschmidt, who constantly niggle at each other in the confines of the sub, each talking in their native tongue yet understanding each other perfectly. More scenes with them would not have been amiss.

As a whole, the cast remain underused and we care little what happens to them, which is never a good thing, even in a slapstick comedy such as this. The film finds its feet when it's at its zaniest, such as when Kelso zooms down Hollywood Boulevard in his Warhwark. The sequence looks akin to Luke Skywalker whizzing along the trench of the Death Star at the climax of *Star Wars*. Whether this is deliberate by Spielberg is a question for the man himself, but it's certainly the first thing that popped into my head.

The score by John Williams, who had already collaborated several times with Spielberg, seems at times as frenetic and out-of-control as the picture itself. If Williams was aiming for this, then he certainly succeeded. But, for me, it's one of his few overtures that does little to enhance the film it's attached to.

Something that hurts *1941*, I think, is that it fails to rein in the cartoonish atmosphere, despite being purportedly based on fact. The comedy is done with broad brushstrokes, and focuses purely on the hysteria gripping the west coast of America six days after the horrific events of Pearl Harbour. But the brushstroke is inconsistent,

WILD BILL WANTS YOU
TO SEE "1941" AT YOUR LOCAL THEATRE

79

since there were too many people contributing to the script and too many disparate acting styles. You almost get the feeling the contributors were trying to out-do each other, each top-trumping the other with the wackiest ideas to put on screen. With all the talent attached, *1941* could and should have been so much more.

If everything is to be believed, Spielberg had the final say, controlling everything from second unit work to model shots. *Everything*. It seems safe to say, therefore, that comedy was not his strong suit at this point in his career. It would be interesting to see what the director could do with the genre today. This piece of filmmaking should only be seen as a learning curve.

If Zemeckis had had more of a say in the proceedings (remember, he was a newcomer channelling his energy into writing, not directing), maybe things would have turned out differently. In later years, both Zemeckis and Gale, when interviewed about the picture, showed an unrepentant attitude. They insist the slapstick and anarchy work just fine; they achieved what they set out to achieve by bringing such epic-scale mayhem to the big screen.

I first saw this picture at my local fleapit when it came out in 1979. My pimpled teenaged hormonal self was none too taken with it at the time. I saw it for the second time three days ago before I took to my laptop to write this article. Do I think the film has aged well? No. In fact, by today's standards it comes across possibly even more racist and bigoted than it did before. I can imagine it offending a wide range of people. We've become sensitive little souls in this modern age of ours, but I was a youth in the '70s and even then I found myself uncomfortable at aspects of the plot, like Tim Matheson's sleazing over Nancy Allen, or Treat Williams lavishing unwanted attention on Dianne Kay. These scenes almost allude to date rape (something which should never be made light of).

I would say the film can be enjoyed it for its set pieces, which at times work very well. But as a whole it is too "in your face" and doesn't know when to put the brakes on. Is it funny? That is subjective and will depend on

the taste in humour of individual viewers. Who am I to decide what is and isn't funny on behalf of a large number of people? Humour doesn't work like that. Make your own mind up, and we can compare notes afterwards!

The saddest thing is that *1941* could have been so much more. I think harsh lessons were learned here, egos were checked, arrogance and self-confidence were shaken. Everyone involved went on to better things, films that won a place in our collective hearts, and it's a pity *1941* isn't among them as, with a little more thought and finesse, it most definitely could have been.

80

THE REVOLUTION OF 1970

by Allen Rubinstein

Joe Tyler, a distinguished, middle-aged, balding man with a moustache, walks purposefully through a college campus while credits come and go in animated bubbles. Folk singer Melanie warbles her impatience on the soundtrack, *"Reason is the only way to change what we're creating, but reason sometimes turns into another word for waiting. You keep right on talking, but I don't want to hear it anymore."* The man encounters a scarecrow effigy hung from a tree with a sign stating: "JOE MUST <u>GO</u>". He turns to face a building marked 'Administration' where around twenty students stare out two rows of windows like they're in the joke wall of *Laugh In*.

President Joe Tyler: What is it this time, Rossiter?

Rossiter: Don't tell me our president can't read.

Dempsey (an African-American student): Dr. Tyler, Rossiter's group and Hudson Afro have occupied this hall to present, um… (*holds up a typewritten page*) twelve demands.

Tyler: I'll hear them when you leave the building.

Rossiter: And we'll state them when you leave the campus.

Estella: Buzz off, Tyler. Pack up your dishrags and go. (*The students laugh generously*).

Dishrags. Apparently, Joe the college president has them and the campus radicals aren't a fan. Dr. Tyler walks away sadly. By the next cut, he's already resigned his position, presumably buzzing off with his prize collection of dishrags. This inciting incident opens *R.P.M.* * **Revolutions*

Per Minute (1970), a little-known feature from Columbia Pictures where long-established Hollywood liberal Stanley Kramer and *Yellow Submarine* screenwriter Erich Segal have decided this is how young people talk and that high-ranking education administrators can be chased away from their livelihoods by being ridiculed about cleaning supplies.

Nobody would confuse Stanley Kramer with the '70s crop of New Hollywood directors. He had credits going back to 1933 and wasn't exactly the voice of the baby boomer generation. *R.P.M.* is his attempt to understand their politics and how he fits in with them. This is probably why it centers around 54 year old Anthony Quinn as Paco, a veteran leftist and sociology professor struggling to communicate with the student groups who are bent on shaking up his employers.

In the wild creative days of 1970, Kramer contributed to a compelling wave of films about the student movement of the late '60s. You could argue it started with cinematographer Haskell Wexler's experimental fiction/documentary hybrid *Medium Cool* (1969) and closed with Peter Watkin's *Punishment Park* and Jack Nicholson's *Drive, He Said* in 1971. In this article, I'll be looking at the core of the cycle, five titles from 1970: *Zabriskie Point, R.P.M., The Strawberry Statement, Getting Straight* and *The Revolutionary*. (Robert Kramer's *ICE* - an obscure black and white polemic - trod similar thematic ground but depicted a fictional revolution in a fictional version of the United States).

I'm aware of no other period of history - save perhaps France's uprisings in 1968 - that produced such a cinematic flurry of portrayals so quickly on the heels of one another. I suppose it's possible the World War II films put out during the war collectively qualify, though with institutional backing and propaganda intentions which made the output as unlike as cultural touchstones could possibly be.

As far as the gatekeepers were concerned, this was an example of chasing youth market dollars by using headlines as their guide, a financial calculation that makes them no less culturally significant. 1970 was the cusp of processing the previous three years of communes, assassinations and Indochina massacres. It was the midpoint between the Summer of Love and Watergate. The protest films represent only a fraction of the counterculture presence in theaters during those years, from *Barbarella* to *Fritz the Cat*. 1970 also saw the release of *Woodstock* and *Gimme Shelter*, polar lodestars of counterculture via its unfiltered language of rock-and-roll. '60s color and optimism were replaced with edgier, less forgiving material that year - *Joe, End of the Road, Deep End, WUSA, Performance* and, of course, *Five Easy Pieces*.

To understand how connected to the history of their time these films were, *Zabriskie Point* came out early February, one week before the Chicago 7 verdicts; *Getting Straight* hit theaters in May, one week after four Kent State students were shot dead and nine wounded by the National Guard, and riots stemming from that incident were still ongoing; *The Strawberry Statement* (and *Joe*) opened in June, shortly before Nixon signed the law lowering the voting age to 18; *The Revolutionary* was released in July, a few weeks before the campaign to free Black Panther

ZABRISKIE POINT

MICHELANGELO ANTONIONI

METRO-GOLDWYN-MAYER présente une PRODUCTION CARLO PONTI "ZABRISKIE POINT"
UN FILM DE **MICHELANGELO ANTONIONI** AVEC **MARK FRECHETTE DARIA HALPRIN** ROD TAYLOR
SCENARIO MICHELANGELO ANTONIONI FRED GARDNER SAM SHEPARD TONINO GUERRA CLARE PEPLOE
MUSIQUE ORIGINALE **PINK FLOYD ROLLING STONES** JERRY GARCIA THE GRATEFUL DEAD THE YOUGBLOODS
DIRECTEUR PHOTO ALFIO CONTINI PRODUCTEUR DELEGUE HARRISSON STARR
UNE DISTRIBUTION MISSION LICENCE HOLLYWOOD CLASSICS LIMITED

Huey Newton concluded with his exoneration and the campaign to free Angela Yvonne Davis began with her arrest. As if to drive home the musical reference in its title, *R.P.M.* came out several days before the death of Jimi Hendrix in September and Janis Joplin a month later, both 27 years old. This chapter of American history was decidedly still in progress.

The very organizing depicted in these films was in a state of pure momentum. They were sketching out drama from a movement that was reaching its zenith months after the scripts were written, even as the elements of its own demise were present, growing and inevitable. Most of their stories are drawn from books that rode the wave of public interest in current events, but even those taken directly from participant accounts can be forgiven a pronounced lack of perspective.

What can we make of them now, fifty-plus years later? Few people watched the movies on their release, and, outside of *Zabriskie Point*'s place in Michelangelo

Antonioni's oeuvre, they're rarely considered today. They're a shaggy, ramshackle collection of films. None of them are completely successful, but none are complete failures either. In current reviews, they're called curios, throwbacks or time capsules - a fair assessment as a blip in the flow of the anti-war, anti-establishment culture of the time, unmistakably flawed, mostly forgotten.

Where they become more interesting is as a comparative study in how and why to fictionalize direct political action. Protest movements are notoriously difficult to make compelling onscreen. They're conflict-based at their root, but the acts of carrying signs, occupying streets and chanting slogans don't themselves build suspense. The goals and results, if any, tend to be conceptual, incremental and spread over many years. The subject is more appropriate to biopics of figures like MLK and Gandhi, whose lifelong efforts made a clearer political and cultural impact than the short-lived burst of activity Nixon, Johnson and Vietnam inspired from 1967 until the war ended.

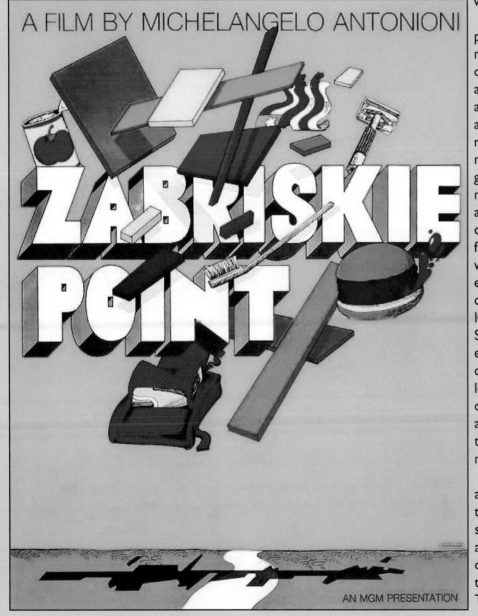

A FILM BY MICHELANGELO ANTONIONI

ZABRISKIE POINT

AN MGM PRESENTATION

At this point, it is useful for me to, as political organizers term it, "credential" myself. I did my time in the trenches during my young-adult years in the '90s and '00s. I held meetings with scrappy activists, campaigned for politicians and ballot measures, worked for reform-minded non-profits, read three newspapers a day, harassed security guards in buildings where board meetings were held twenty floors above, and loudly declared my staunch opposition to the death penalty in front of nobody in particular. Having worked for and against a variety of establishments, I can say with as much certainty as anyone born in 1968 that Kramer, Antonioni, Richard Rush, Stuart Hagmann and Paul Williams exhibited a degree of verisimilitude on their collective topic. I know the lefties in these protest groups - their dreams and fantasies, their strengths and limitations. They revere the era of the '60s, and they haven't changed that much.

For example, let's return to *R.P.M.* and its sudden dishrag deficiency. In all the public and private reaction to the student movement, I'm not aware of any instance where faculty was let go or abandoned the profession, much less the resignation of a college president. The Board of Trustees state: "We're

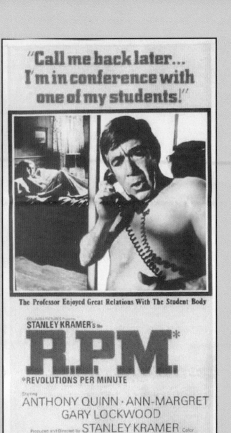

"Call me back later...
I'm in conference with
one of my students!"

The Professor Enjoyed Great Relations With The Student Body

COLUMBIA PICTURES presents
STANLEY KRAMER'S film
R.P.M.
*REVOLUTIONS PER MINUTE
Starring
ANTHONY QUINN · ANN-MARGRET
GARY LOCKWOOD
Produced and Directed by STANLEY KRAMER Color
Written by ERICH SEGAL
Music by BARRY DE VORZON and PERRY BOTKIN, JR.

in trouble", and refer to the student group's list of preferred replacements. The list of three comprises deceased revolutionary Che Guevara, the Black Panther Eldridge Cleaver and the film's protagonist sociology professor F.W.J. 'Paco' Perez. The trustees hire Paco as acting president because he can communicate and negotiate with the students. Evacuating them from the administration building seems to be the trustees' solitary concern in running their college.

Newly appointed, Paco surveys the occupiers' list of 12 demands. "No military research. Well, nothing wrong with them apples," Paco says, tossing aside any staff or financial commitments the college may have. At this point, Rossiter (Gary Lockwood) and the Hudson Afro group (represented by Paul Winfield) are the most successful and powerful campus political group in the history of the United States. An issue comes up over recruiting a black Board of Trustee member, since they have only one black alumna, but the Board agrees to the first nine of the twelve items, including an inner-city scholarship program, a campus investment program and disinvestment in stocks of businesses that operate in South Africa. Instead of popping open bottles of champagne, the group refuses the offer and holds out for the final three - undefined participation in hiring and firing of faculty, granting of degrees and the writing of curriculum to reflect the issues of the day. The stalemate builds to the police confrontation at the climax of the film.

It's pure fantasyland. If Kramer hadn't established his political bonafides in previous projects, you might mistake this for a conservative hack job, with activists portrayed as spoiled, angry children creating chaos for perfectly reasonable, acquiescent education leaders. I suspect, with the protagonist being an old union man and Kramer himself from a working-class background, this is the template for their ideas about how political action works. Unions can legitimately and quickly interfere with the operation of a workplace when they are minded to do so. Rando activists find it hard to be more than gadflies under the best of circumstances. It's everything a group can do just to be taken seriously as a force, something the mid-thirties-aged college students in *R.P.M.* seem to command simply by existing. In a real-life school building occupation, the officials would just let them wait it out until lack of food and bathing or plain boredom caused them to abandon the takeover.

COLUMBIA PICTURES Presents
STANLEY KRAMER's film of
R.P.M.
*REVOLUTIONS PER MINUTE
Starring
ANTHONY QUINN · ANN-MARGRET · GARY LOCKWOOD
Written by ERICH SEGAL Music by BARRY DE VORZON and PERRY BOTKIN, JR.
Produced and Directed by STANLEY KRAMER Color

It's worth wondering what the purpose is of making these films. Principles of organizing say you create media for the purposes of radicalization and recruitment, but here that seems unlikely. Most of the groups depicted and their specific actions lack context - the context that was sitting right outside the theater doors - and political expression across the board is watered down and generic. Signs among a protest merely allude to fighting the draft, but nobody raises the issue. Race is mentioned, but rarely explored in any depth. If you watch the documentaries shot during this era showing hippie gatherings or protests, the participants are far smarter and more engaged than the characters in these films. They have a strength of conviction and coherent systemic critique that the movies lack.

Stuart Hagmann's *The Strawberry Statement* comes closest since it's adapted from the memoir of a participant. Bruce Davison plays Simon, the film's stand-in for James Simon Kunen who wrote about his involvement with the Columbia occupation of their administration building. Davison's Simon wanders into the protest already in progress

to meet girls but becomes politicized as the story progresses. One of the motivations for their sit-in is the university's takeover of a local park and community center, mostly used by the town's minority population. They intend to use the land as an ROTC training facility, but one activist finds paperwork that reveals their deal with power company Western Pacific and Electric. The college will hold the land tax free until the corporation builds a high rise; meanwhile the company's Chairman of the Board is also a trustee. This is great material - based on a similar scandal when students occupied at Columbia - but in the movie, the scheme is something of an afterthought. The community losing their playground is never seen nor heard from, and the activists seem barely connected to the issue.

After Simon's friend has his leg broken by "jocks" while the police

stand and watch (all off screen), Davison spills some of the passion he's been building to the school secretary, the only person in the administration who will listen to him:

"There are plenty of other legs and arms around here to break, lady, and unless this school gives the building and the playground back to the neighborhood, unless this school gives some room to some jet-black faces around here, unless this school gives up its war research program, unless this school gives up the fucking nineteenth century and calls off the pigs, it's gonna be all over. Now you've been hearing about revolution, right? You've been watching it on the television, reading it in the newspaper? Well, it's not there, it's here! Here! In every toilet in this idiot school there's a kid waiting for tonight, and unless you

call off the pigs, it's gonna be a mess and war. And not because it has to be, but because you started it."

Those are strong words in any era. For 1970, they're incendiary, and the film has the imagery to match as it marches to its violent climax. I know I'm damning it with faint praise, but *The Strawberry Statement* understands where students were at the time better than a crusty studio production like *R.P.M.*, which is mostly about an old liberal's fear of being left behind.

In part, the scattershot politics in these political films is because of the scattershot politics of young protest groups. Activists in real life can't focus down to potentially achievable issues, perpetually carry the blinders of their own socio-economic upbringings, and spend far too much time and energy butting heads with authority figures rather than what they want to change and how to influence political targets to change it. It's particularly unsatisfying in a film context since by necessity, each movie drops you directly into the action without all the leafletting, meetings, ideological debates and speeches, and the institutional conflicts over leadership and strategy. Those things would not only be nearly impossible to dramatize, they would make any film dreadfully dull, yet looking into the histories of groups like the Students for a Democratic Society, that's the work; it's what gets them to the protest lines. Abbie Hoffman, asked during the criminal trial against the Chicago 7 whether they agreed to overthrow the U.S. government, responded: "We couldn't agree on lunch." It makes you wonder if shooting fictional films that mirror the work of these organizations is fundamentally a bad idea.

Richard Rush's *Getting Straight* not only doesn't seem to grasp the nuances of political activists, it's got some peculiar ideas about human behavior in general. Rush and screenwriters Ken Kolb and Robert Kaufman had a background in Roger Corman biker films and screwball comedies, so the intensity from *The Strawberry Statement* is turned up to eleven. Add in Elliot Gould's character having a screamy emotional crisis played against Candice Bergen's usual mannered performance, and *Getting Straight* is a very strange movie. Their campus rebellion isn't an organized political action as much as a force of nature unleashed. It starts with circles of a dozen protestors carrying generic signs and builds to a frenzy of destruction, with seemingly every student on campus destroying desks with axes. Gould watches a black power activist run down a corridor with a crazed look in his eye, breaking random windows with a hammer, and they exchange smiles of approval and recognition. The other films see frustration in the inability to make change; *Getting Straight* sees a cauldron of seething rage.

Gould tries to warn them. An administrator goes to him to present a counterproposal - some compromises the school wants to make in response to protestors'

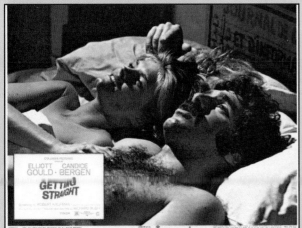

political demands. Nobody in the film has bothered to mention these demands, or even that there are demands, before this scene begins; they are just suddenly important. The professor's proffers are weak tea, condescending half-measures, and Gould predictably loses his mind. "It's too late for those kind of answers! You'll drive them crazy, Dr. Vandenberg! They'll burn down your school! You are turning them into full-scale revolutionaries!" *The Strawberry Statement* soft-pedals its politics, but it at least knows enough to show politicization as a process and a personal journey. Here, everything is stimuli-based, like a sociology experiment where those taking deliberate action lack agency and self-knowledge.

Gould plays an older student, Harry Bailey, struggling to cross the finish line of his Masters degree so he can teach high school. He used to be the campus radical before getting drafted to Vietnam; now he just wants to lie low, study and get laid, even though the others keep trying to pull him back into the fray.

Getting Straight contributes a perspective on politics outside the campus, something missing in *R.P.M.* and *Strawberry*'s hermetically sealed conflicts.

In one of his many speeches, Gould takes down a strategy meeting: "It's a good safe target... The campus where it's safe to measure ding-a-lings with the establishment because they let you. Why protest on the campus? Why not protest out in the real world where it'll do some good? Want to hand out draft tips? Forget about college kids; they'll take care of themselves. Set your booth outside a munitions factory, where those poor, ignorant suckers don't stand a chance. Of course, you just might get your teeth kicked in for your troubles."

He then recants and tells them to go fight their fights if they leave him out of it. Gould has marched in Selma, and he's committed only to self-seeking now, until the bone-headed conservatism of the system and the outlandish response of the student body drive him to sabotage everything he's worked for. It's a mad collision of mixed messages, presenting a stark binary choice between calcified institutions of academia, consumerism and marriage or, apparently, breaking stuff with a large mallet.

It's that last step which bewilders the filmmakers as much as the activists. You can rip through the establishment, tear down false dreams and fake national pride, expose the violence inherent in the system, you can even get the attention of the powerful with enough people and enough commotion, but then what? The excellent 1990 documentary *Berkeley in the Sixties* films a great illustration of this kind of frustration. Protestors work for weeks, pulling out one strategy after another to disrupt the shipping of drafted soldiers to Vietnam... and achieve nothing. Not a single conscript turns away from his assignment; no government office is deterred or delayed. Those interviewed, with decades between then and now, are still bewildered. How do you stop an evil happening right in front of you? Nobody seems to listen or care; you can only stare in wonder at your lack of power to affect things.

The Revolutionary and to some extent *Zabriskie Point* not only seem to understand this dynamic, they don't shy away from the brain power it takes to arrive at that point of cognitive dissonance. Antonioni's *Zabriskie Point* is a gorgeous film by a great filmmaker which completes its political material in its first half hour. The students in the opening meeting are whip-smart, debating with some black revolutionaries if white people have the right to call themselves that. The unnamed protagonist declares himself bored and leaves, and they immediately discuss the importance of meetings in a revolution. It's almost satirical.

The young man arms himself, then witnesses a dual shooting of a police officer and a protestor in a campus protest he isn't even a part of. The fear puts him on the run. Like any Antonioni film, it's more meditation than polemic, and quite possibly the most anti-American film ever released by a major studio. The portrayal of the current politics is authentic and engaging, and it frames the critique of capitalism and culture that follows, if

only to say that standing against that system can get you killed.

Finally, director Paul Williams (not the diminutive singer/songwriter) casts Jon Voight as *The Revolutionary*, a film from Hans Konigsberger's novel. Known only as 'A', Voight is a poor intellectual somewhat lost in his head and philosophy as a member of a university political group called the Radical Committee. They attempt to raise a fuss at a rally but are arrested before they get out two sentences. Voight writes an impassioned message to the judge on toilet paper, then is tossed to the street without being brought before anyone. He goes to confront an administrator who refers to him and his colleagues as "nice young people". This last embarrassment prompts him to quit the Radical Committee calling them "a bunch of old ladies." He's tired of

the books and tired of the theories. He wants to get something done.

The film takes him on a sharp, intriguing journey, even if as the story it is light on real drama. His next stop is the Central Committee, led by Robert Duvall, a working class Marxist-Leninist collective clinging to their jobs at the town factory. They take him in, saying: "We can use him. He's got a nice bourgeois, liberal face." Voigt breaks his back making cheap mimeographs with a broken typewriter and leafletting people who hurl abuse at him. The Central Committee gets bogged down in bureaucracy and in-fighting. He falls for a sweet rich girl and sees how little he fits into that world even as she starts to admire his motives. He's drafted, goes AWOL, then lives in hiding in the rich girl's garden house. Finally, he connects with a loose crew who engage in direct, militant civil disobedience. They paint on walls, break into a pawn shop and give away the merchandise, and plan

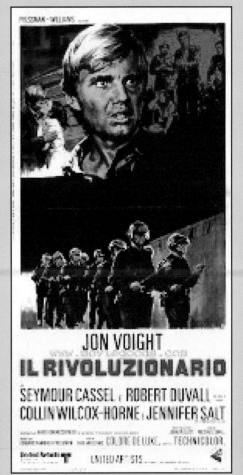

terrorist attacks. It's interesting to note all these factions demonstrate open disdain for one another. The film ends on a freeze frame, with "A" deciding whether or not to step over the line from quiet, ineffectual revolutionary thinker to blowing up a judge. Gunshots are heard softly on the soundtrack.

The Revolutionary is the slowest and least energetic of these movies - the most considered, the most thoughtful and the least known (it took me years to find it). It contains a familiar narrative for those who watch the news then or today. No matter the issue or the tactics involved, leftist action is always tarred with fears and accusations of violence - whether real, exaggerated or imaginary. What will these people do? How far will they go? The Panthers' photo shoots with long rifles struck terrible fear in the hearts of white suburbanites (while their many community services were ignored), raising far more concern than the hot death being rained daily on a third world population

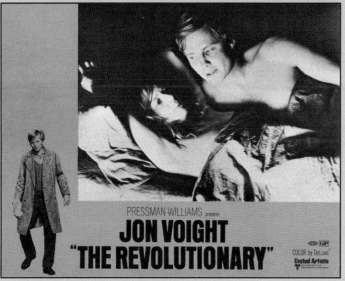

thousands of miles away.

However, the leftists ask themselves the exact same questions. Will they be ignored, or should they make sure they are impossible to ignore? The vast majority of activists remain firmly in the camp of non-violent dissent, but Voight's journey is not that far outside the box. (There's an excellent film from 1974 called *Bingo*, a Canadian version of *The Revolutionary*, following much the same path for its young activist). Part of the dissolution of the Students for Democratic Society was a faction breaking away to become The Weathermen, whose biggest action caused $300,000 (in 1970s dollars) of damage in Washington, DC. Thing is, for all the soul-rending it takes to make it to that point - SDS was torn apart by it - the bombs didn't topple the system either. Very shortly, a group of Weathermen accidentally blew themselves up with their own explosives, and many of their leaders ended up on the run for decades.

Did these movies matter? They're a fascinating record, if nothing else. With all that works and doesn't work, you could mash them together and make one great, classic movie. They're an example of the challenges and contradictions of combining radical politics with commercial filmmaking. Not only are there places directors and writers are simply not permitted to go with the millions they need from their own capitalists, there's a built-in problem with perspective. One of the things *R.P.M.* gets right is that it identifies that a successful political action hinges on power - who has it and what it means to wield it. Quinn's Paco isn't corrupt, but by taking on the powerful role of school president, he's accountable. An entire institution and everyone who depends on it is impacted by the decisions he makes. He doesn't have the freedom to join the students in their quixotic drive for their own power, which is what their last three demands call for. He has responsibilities to the school and its resources. The same is true for producers and executives at a studio. They aren't likely to fully understand the point of view of those who are invisible to the media, but they do know that none of these films recouped their costs.

All that said, nothing that can honestly be called "the revolution" really happened; racism, poverty, and all the other ills the movement fought against are still with us in force. There are those who declare with confidence that the anti-war movement ended the war. Public support of the Vietnam incursion dropped from 61% in 1965 to 31% in 1971, which restricts what leadership can get away with. The reasons are so many - Kronkite, the Pentagon Papers, My Lai, the draft, general fatigue. All throughout, the students and their allies were marching, leafletting, organizing and drawing the attention of the media. All throughout, the movies were there, part of the stew that made Nixon pull those troops out of harm's way and stop murdering Southeast Asians for war profiteers.

It's important here that I add one more film to this analysis. We shouldn't close without at least one true record of what really happened. *FTA* is a documentary of an unbelievable road show. Jane Fonda, Donald Sutherland and six other players put together a collection of biting skits, anti-war songs both funny and serious, and a few short speeches and performed the show outside military bases in the US and the Pacific Rim. FTA stands for "Fuck the Army". At the revue's conclusion, they openly advocate for soldiers to refuse their missions and engage in collective disobedience. Between shows, they held meetings where soldiers could share their experience of helplessness, trauma and racism. Attendance at these shows was prohibited, but venues were full anyway. You have just got to admire the stones. This is what effective activism looks like.

This documentary was just as embroiled in history as all the rest. *FTA* was released in July, 1972, just as Fonda arrived for her controversial visit to North Vietnam (she and her husband, the leader and founder of Students for a Democratic Society, Tom Hayden, had sponsored trips there for several years). She visited sites where mines had destroyed the Red River dike system that farmers depended on. She was also photographed on a North Vietnamese anti-aircraft weapon, earning her the nickname 'Hanoi

Jane' and the lifelong loathing of certain Vietnam veterans. The trip was inflammatory enough that the White House made calls to distributor American International Pictures (AIP), who pulled *FTA* out of theaters after less than a week of showings and then incinerated every print of the film they could get their hands on. The documentary was only available in bootleg form until its restoration in 2009.

The movie includes electrifying footage of Fonda testifying before the Foreign Correspondent's Club, speaking without notes at a rapid clip: "It is our responsibility, all of us, from whatever country we come from to recognize that, although there are fewer grunts, ground troops, paeons, snuffies, whatever you want to call them in Vietnam, fewer white American soldiers dying, there are more yellow people dying than ever before because of the defoliants that we're dropping, the chemicals that we're using, the bomb tonnage that we're using, the types of new kinds of sophisticated automated battlefield mechanisms that are being put into Vietnam. I'm sure that you all know that as well as we do. Over two-and-a-half times Hiroshima is being dropped in terms of bomb tonnage on Laos, Cambodia and Vietnam each week. Two-and-a-half times Hiroshima. That's a terrifying thing to recognize, that there are babies being born with flippers instead of hands, with soft skulls, with no tear ducts, with soft palates because of the things our government are dropping on that country. Their crops are being destroyed; their animals are being destroyed; their water supply is being polluted. There are areas where people will never be able to live again and it's our government doing it - the American government in our names. The soldiers know this. The soldiers that are loading the bombs into planes know it. The soldiers that are working on the flight lines know it. The pilots know it. The photo reconnaissance experts know it. The men who are waging the war, from Okinawa, from Japan, from the Philippines, from Hawaii, from the nuclear attack aircraft carriers - they know it. And they're beginning to say no. We will not load bombs anymore. We will not kill Vietnamese people anymore. And we're beginning to ask ourselves why and in whose interests are we here."

In this documentary, there are no games, supercilious professors, distracting flirtation or histrionic graduate students. There are no dishrags - just pure, unadulterated truth and people with the courage to speak it directly into the face of power.

Did these movies matter? Hell, yes, they did. They mattered a lot.

For every flaw and bit of silliness in them, they were a clarion voice in a political culture of mass moral outrage that hasn't been spoken at such volume or with such unity ever since. Every contribution, every word spoken in service to expressing that outrage mattered, whether it was heard by thirty, thirty thousand or three million. The very act of creating this collection of tales - the thousands involved for months or years in creating large, expensive examples of energetic dissent - more than justifies their existence. The people who made these films believed in them, and we should do everything to honor that. It's a gathering of energy and power that we desperately need today.

THE SHOW THE PENTAGON COULDN'T STOP!
Here in all its wit and anger is the explosive entertainment that matched the talents of Jane Fonda, Donald Sutherland and the F.T.A. Troupe against the power of the Pentagon, filmed where it happened, while it happened.

FREE THEATRE ASSOCIATES Presents A DUQUE FILMS, INC. Production
JANE FONDA   DONALD SUTHERLAND
MICHAEL ALAIMO · LEN CHANDLER · PAMALA DONEGAN
RITA MARTINSON · PAUL MOONEY · HOLLY NEAR · YALE ZIMMERMAN
in "F.T.A."
Produced By FRANCINE PARKER JANE FONDA DONALD SUTHERLAND Directed by FRANCINE PARKER Background Score: AMINADAV ALONI
Written By: MICHAEL ALAIMO, LEN CHANDLER, PAMALA DONEGAN, ROBIN MENKEN, RITA MARTINSON, HOLLY NEAR and DALTON TRUMBO.
In COLOR An AMERICAN INTERNATIONAL Release

Rebel Yell

CAGED HEAT!

by Julian Hobbs

In 1971, legendary director Roger Corman, tired of studio meddling, threw all his eggs into his own recently formed production company New World Pictures. Deciding to take a temporary hiatus from directing (which lasted for eighteen years), Corman hired enthusiastic, hungry-for-success young students - some straight out of UCLA - to do the hard work for him... for less pay! The list of directors that successfully graduated from Corman's New World film school reads like a who's who of Hollywood notables: Allan Arkush, John Sayles, Ron Howard, Joe Dante, Martin Scorsese, James Cameron, Curtis Hanson, Stephanie Rothman, Jonathan Kaplan and, of course, future Oscar-winning director Jonathan Demme.

Regarded as the most versatile and enthusiastic of Corman's young staffers at New World, Demme had written and produced their 'chicks-in-chains' movie *The Hot Box* in 1972. It was shot in the Philippines (exotic locations and next-to-nothing production costs made the country a hotbed of filmmaking activity in the '70s) and Demme earned his spurs overseeing all aspects of the turbulent production, including directing the second unit.

Buoyed by the experience, Demme pushed Corman to give him a directorial shot. The New World supremo said yes, but stipulated he wanted Demme to deliver a workable script for another 'women-in-prison' opus. Some might have regarded the assignment as a poison chalice, but Demme approached it with typical professionalism, delivering a workable screenplay in double-quick time and willingly accepting Corman's suggestions for script revisions and improvements. He was the first debuting director to receive the soon-to-be mandatory pre-shoot

pep talk from the mogul.

Corman felt a good exploitation flick should grab the viewer by the lapels from the opening moments. *Caged Heat* certainly does, opening with a shootout between cops and drug dealers which results in several deaths. Jackie (Erica Gavin), the girlfriend of one of the shooters, is caught and receives a harsh ten-year prison sentence, just the first of many unjust punishments in the movie. She is incarcerated at a tough female prison run by the authoritarian Warden McQueen ('60s horror queen Barbara Steele). In time honoured prison movie style, Jackie takes a brave stand against the warden while making an enemy of the prison's toughest inmate, Maggie (Juanita Brown).

Later, the warden is offended by an entertainment evening staged by Belle (Roberta Collins) and Pandora (Ella Reid) in which they dress up as men and delight the audience with lewd jokes. The prudish McQueen singles out the more rebellious Pandora for punishment, sentencing her to two days in the hole on starvation rations. The increasingly barbaric and unfair punishment only succeeds in uniting the inmates against their captors. In response, McQueen ups the ante by instructing the sexually deviant prison doctor to carry out electric shock therapy and lobotomies on the most troublesome inmates. After being unfairly accused of staging a prison break, Jackie and Maggie are subjected to grueling electric shock treatment. They vow to put their differences aside, and successfully stage a daring break from a prison detail.

This last third of the picture moves some of the action away from the oppressive confines of the prison, allowing

Demme to lighten the tone somewhat and mix in more crowd-pleasing comedy and action. This is where *Caged Heat* delivers on its 'Renegade Women' original production moniker. Stealing police cars, duffing up vice cops and staging bank raids are all in a day's work for Jackie, Maggie and their new companion, the aptly named Crazy (Lynda Gold), who, following the closure of a local factory, is left with little option than to take a job in a glorified brothel. Injustice reigns, inside and outside the prison walls, and the girls haven't forgotten about their friends languishing behind bars.

The Corman recipe for New World box-office success had to be rigidly adhered to by his directors. The formula was straightforward. Get as much exploitable sex and violence onscreen as possible, mix with a dash of comedy, and season with an anti-authoritarian, liberal message so that college kids and twenty-somethings (who made up most of the potential audience) could cheer along while lapping up the titillating thrills.

But even Corman had some moral scruples about making 'women-in-prison' flicks, considered one of the most disreputable of all exploitation subgenres. While *Caged Heat* undoubtedly ticks all the sleazy boxes associated with the form - gratuitous shower scenes, sadistic prison guards, catfights between inmates, victimisation of prisoners, and so on - there is also a progressive political message and anti-authoritarian vibe at play. These distinguish it from, say, the more crushingly downbeat movies Jesus Franco was churning out with monotonous regularity at the time.

By contrast, *Caged Heat* is a freewheeling, exciting exploitation picture which offers a feminist viewpoint and expresses it in a more committed, crowd-pleasing way than other Corman 'women-in-prison' flicks. Take *The Big Doll House,* which had kicked the cycle off in the first place and been a massive box office success. In this, that rebellious spirit is certainly evident, but that's more attributable to the sheer screen presence of star Pam Grier than the script or filmmakers. *Caged Heat,* by accident or design, feels like a genuinely subversive work.

Backed by a highly capable production crew, Demme directs with confidence and verve. Providing perfect support, cinematographer Tak Fujimoto (look for his walk-on-walk-off cameo as a brothel customer) - a key confidante of the director throughout his long and successful career - employs a handheld camera to vividly capture the desperation of the inmates in their darkest moments. Elegant panning shots show the inmates going about their daily business, providing a believable picture of the day-to-day drudgery of prison life, allowing the audience to keep tabs on the drama's major players, who are many, as befits the egalitarian nature of the piece. Meanwhile, that all-important Corman-requested nudity is undoubtedly plentiful. But Demme generally captures such moments in static mid-shot while the inmates go

about their daily routine. It becomes just another facet of the dehumanising prison experience rather than titillating in any way.

By moving the genre away from the banana republic setting of *The Big Doll House* and its offshoots back to North America, the political points (both satirical and serious) hit much closer to home. These digs are about as subtle as a sledgehammer but they hit the mark. Warden McQueen conducts her kangaroo court under a proudly displayed American flag with a photo of the then-president 'Tricky Dicky' Nixon looking down benignly on some of the more depraved business!

Despite these broad strokes, Steele's McQueen, the true villain of the piece, is not of the comic book variety. A surprisingly poignant scene captures her sad and lonely existence, struggling from a wheelchair and sleeping alone in a bare office. She gazes at a picture of herself in her younger days, standing next to her mother and father. Whether she is looking back with nostalgia to a happy childhood long gone or remembering darker experiences is left open to question by Demme. Critic Danny Peary, whose excellent tome 'Cult Movies' provides a thorough overview of the film, connects this scene to the ambivalent final shot of Polanski's *Repulsion*.

It's all in the eye of the beholder, of course, but the notion that McQueen was perhaps abused by her father provides a psychological rationale for her repressive punishment regime. Demme takes the Freudian implications further, staging a remarkable dream sequence in which McQueen - clad in fishnets, wearing a top hat, and swinging a cane - performs a song and dance number wherein she berates the inmates for their promiscuous ways! Punchily effective dream sequences are employed to expose the innermost fears and desires of the inmates, too.

Never vamping it up, Steele's warden is unerringly polite yet completely unreasonable; an all too human 'monster' who reminded me of - and predates - Louise Fletcher's unforgettable Nurse Ratchet from the acclaimed *One Flew Over the Cuckoo's Nest* (1975). There are also strong echoes of the Ken Kesey novel/Milos Forman classic in the theme of lobotomy and electric shock therapy employed to control rebellious inmates.

More cut and dried are the rambunctious characterizations by the likes of Russ Meyer's fave Erica Gavin, talented ingenue Rainbeaux Smith and blaxploitation staple Juanita Brown. They have a blast with their roles, delighting in turning the tables on the incompetent, lackadaisical men of authority they encounter while defiantly standing up for the rights of their 'sisters.' In one audaciously mounted set piece, the fugitives stage an armed bank robbery only to find a gang of male criminals are in the process of doing the same! Demme deftly fuses comedy, action and bloody violence here to typically exhilarating effect.

The climax pulls a similar trick, where the drama appears to be heading for a *Bonnie and Clyde/Butch Cassidy and the Sundance Kid*-style downbeat conclusion. The gang, heavily outnumbered, is ambushed by armed prison guards. That feeling is reinforced by Demme, who deftly employs slow motion and still frames when the gunfire starts, upping the excitement a further notch. Instead, the director turns expectations on their head by closing the movie on an upbeat note while also making a blackly comic point at the stupidity of gun-toting authority figures.

When released Stateside in 1974, *Caged Heat* earned surprisingly good reviews from savvy movie critics who praised its cinematic brio and rebellious spirit. Unfortunately, this didn't translate to box office success. Maybe it was just a little too radical and rebellious for a mainstream American audience. Or, just as likely, Corman had killed the goose that laid the golden egg by flooding the market with similar pictures. In any case, its relative financial failure didn't curtail Demme's meteoric rise as a director, and Corman - who loved making money but was still an artist at heart - was genuinely pleased by the critical response. As Demme's star rose, so did *Caged Heat*'s. It went on to be screened at the Museum of Modern Art.

Demme never forgot the part Corman played in getting his directorial career off the ground, later awarding his mentor small but significant roles in the Oscar-winning films *The Silence of the Lambs* (1991) and *Philadelphia* (1995). These turns, alongside books and documentaries focusing on his '60s and '70s output, kept Corman's name in the public eye as he bravely soldiered on in the ever-changing low-budget film production arena. When he finally received that well-deserved Lifetime Achievement Award Oscar in 2009, Demme was, of course, on hand to present the statuette.

DIE HÖLLE TOBT IM HÄRTESTEN FRAUENGEFÄNGNIS DER WELT

DAS ZUCHTHAUS DER VERLORENEN MÄDCHEN

BARBARA STEELE · ROBERTA COLLINS · ERICA GAVIN · JUANITA BROWN
WARREN MILLER · MICKEY FOX · Regie JONATHAN DEMME
Eine Roger Corman Farbfilmproduktion der MONAREX im Verleih

(Many thanks to Mr. Ray Gregory and Mr. Mark Berry for their help assembling this article).

95

Original Artwork by the Students of Confetti Institute of Creative Technologies

Confetti is a specialist creative technology education provider in Nottingham, England, dealing in fimmaking and VFX, video game design and game art, music production and live performance. The following artwork is original work produced specially for this magazine by students aged 17-18 years.

Alien by James Disney

Alien by Kenny Lycett

The Exorcist by Jesse Byrne

Star Wars by Nathan Dobson

Caricatures by Aaron Stielstra

Elliott Gould in *Getting Straight* (pg. 81)

Barbara Steele in *Caged Heat* (pg. 92)

CLOSING CREDITS

James Aaron

James is an American writer and film lover living in Kentucky with his wife and two dogs. He is the author (as Aaron Saylor) of three novels, including 'Sewerville' and 'Adventures in Terror', the latter of which is set during the horror movie and video store boom of the 1980s.

Simon J. Ballard

Simon lives in Oxford and works in its oldest building, a Saxon Tower. Whilst also working in the adjoining church, he has never felt tempted to re-enact scenes from *Taste the Blood of Dracula* or *Dracula A.D.1972*. He has never done this. Ever. He regularly contributes to the magazine 'We Belong Dead' and its various publications, and once read Edgar Allan Poe's 'The Black Cat' to a garden full of drunk young people at his local gay pub The Jolly Farmers. His first published work was a Top Tip in 'Viz' of which he is justifiably proud.

Rachel Bellwoar

Rachel is a writer for 'Comicon', 'Diabolique' magazine and 'Flickering Myth'. If she could have any director fim a biopic about her life it would be Aki Kaurismäki.

David Michael Brown

David is a British ex-pat living in Sydney. Working as a freelance writer he has contributed to 'The Big Issue', 'TV Week', 'GQ', 'Rolling Stone' and 'Empire Magazine Australia', where he was Senior Editor for almost eight years. He is presently writing a book on the film music of German electronic music pioneers Tangerine Dream and researching the work of Andy Warhol associate and indie filmmaker Paul Morrissey for a forthcoming project.

James Cadman

James first discovered his love of films as a child in the 1980s, happily scanning the shelves of his local video shop. Into his 20s, as part of his media degree, he secured work experience with a major film company which included visiting the set of *Notting Hill* at Shepperton Studios. Now living in Derbyshire with his wife and two young children, James enjoys watching and researching films, especially the '70s work of Eastwood, Friedkin, Peckinpah and Scorsese.

Martin Dallard

Fed on a staple diet of the *Six Million Dollar Man*, repeats of the Adam West *Batman* show and the likes of the *Flashing Blade*, and *Champion the Wonder Horse* from a young age, it's no wonder that Martin is self-confessed geek for all things '70s. And whatever you do, don't get him started on the likes of Ron Ely's Doc Savage, as you'll never hear the end of it. Whether it travelled in a TARDIS, or it rode in a red double decker bus, he watched it. But rest assured he never switched off his television set and went and did something less boring instead...

David Flack

David was born and bred in Cambridge. He has had reviews published in 'We Belong Dead' and 'Cinema of the '80s'. He loves watching, talking, reading and writing about film and participating on film forums. The best film he has seen in over 55 years of watching is *Jaws* (1975). The worst is *The Creeping Terror* (1963) or anything by Andy Milligan.

John Harrison

John is a Melbourne, Australia-based freelance writer and film historian who has written for numerous genre publications, including 'Fatal Visions', 'Cult Movies', 'Is It Uncut?', 'Monster!' and 'Weng's Chop'. Harrison is also the author of the Headpress book 'Hip Pocket Sleaze: The Lurid World of Vintage Adult Paperbacks', has recorded audio commentaries for Kino Lorber, and composed the booklet essays for the Australian Blu-ray releases of *Thirst*, *Dead Kids* and *The Survivor*. 'Wildcat!', Harrison's book on the film and television career of former child evangelist Marjoe Gortner, was published by Bear Manor in 2020.

Julian Hobbs

Julian's lifelong love of scary movies began when he was 5 or 6, after being severely traumatized by a TV screening of George Pal's *War of the Worlds*. Several decades later later, Mark Berry asked him to contribute some DVD reviews to his 'Naked' magazine (no, not that kind of mag...) and the film writing bug caught him. He has written for 'We Belong Dead' and its various book offshoots. If he wasn't writing, he'd be beating the skins quite loudly in various Bristol bands. Julian is currently employed within the private health sector after a stint supporting the NHS.

Kev Hurst

Kev is a Nottingham FE college teacher of film and animation and a historian of all things cinematic. He is a massive physical film and TV collector who spends way too much time browsing the shelves of his local CEX store. He is an avid fan of all genres but has passionate interests in all things horror and sci-fi related, from body horror to giallo, dystopian fiction to steampunk. His favourite filmmakers are basically all 'The Movie Brats' and well-respected horror directors like John Carpenter, David Cronenberg, John Landis, Dario Argento, Mario Bava, Tobe Hooper and George A. Romero.

James Lecky

James is an actor, writer and occasional stand-up comedian who has had a lifelong obsession with cinema, beginning with his first visit to the Palace Cinema in Derry (now long since gone) to see *Chitty Chitty Bang Bang* when he was six. Since then, he has happily wallowed in cinema of all kinds but has a particular fondness for Hammer movies, spaghetti westerns, Euro-crime and samurai films.

Bryan C. Kuriawa

Based in New Jersey, Bryan has spent many years diving into the world of movies. Introduced to the Three Stooges by his grandfather and Japanese cinema when he was eight, he's wandered on his own path, ignoring popular opinions. Willing to discuss and defend everything from Jesus Franco's surreal outings to the 007 masterpiece *Moonraker*, nothing is off-limits. Some of his favorite filmmakers include Ishiro Honda, Jacques Tati, Lewis Gilbert, Jesus Franco and Jun Fukuda.

Allen Rubinstein

Allen grew up in an upper-middle-class neighborhood in suburban Connecticut. He writes about movies and history and tries to reveal the truth wherever possible. He works with his wife on a teaching organization called The Poetry Salon (www.thepoetrysalon.com) in Costa Rica while taking care of far too many cats. He has not yet told his parents that he's an anarcho-syndicalist.

Peter Sawford

Peter was born in Essex in 1964 so considers himself a child of the '70s. A self-confessed film buff, he loves watching, reading about and talking about cinema. A frustrated writer his whole life, he's only recently started submitting what he writes to magazines. His favourite director is Alfred Hitchcock with Billy Wilder running him a close second. He still lives in Essex with his wife and works as an IT trainer and when not watching films he's normally panicking over who West Ham are playing next.

Aaron Stielstra

Aaron was born in Ann Arbor, Michigan and grew up in Tucson, AZ. and NYC. He is an actor, writer, illustrator, soundtrack composer and director. After moving to Italy in 2012, he has appeared in 4 spaghetti westerns and numerous horror-thrillers - all of them unnecessarily wet. He recently directed the punk rock comedy *Excretion: the Shocking True Story of the Football Moms*. His favorite '70s actor is Joe Spinell.

Ian Talbot Taylor

After early short story successes, Ian began editing music fanzines and spent decades acting, directing and adjudicating in amateur theatre for the Greater Manchester Drama Federation. He writes for 'The Dark Side', 'Infinity', 'Scream', 'Fantastic Fifties', 'Halls of Horror' and 'We Belong Dead' (and is on the editorial team of the latter). His book on the films of Jenny Agutter appeared in 2021. Ian has progressed from 'prose dabbler' to prolific fiction writer, contributing to and co-editing the BHF Books of Horror. He recently released the collaborative fiction collection 'Spoken in Whispers' and also presents shows for Radio M29 .

Dr. Andrew C. Webber

Dr. W. has been a Film, Media and English teacher and examiner for over 35 years and his passion for the cinema remains undiminished all these years later. As far as he is concerned, a platform is where you wait for the 08.16 to Victoria; dropping is something that louts do with litter; and streaming is how you might feel if you were in *Night of the Hunter* being hotly pursued by Robert Mitchum with "Hate" tattooed on his knuckles and Stanley Cortez doing the cinematography.

Printed in Great Britain
by Amazon

24542372R00059